To Christine and Tony

with best wishes

Malcolm Leslie

FOREST VISION

Transforming the Forestry Commission

Roderick Leslie

Forest Vision
First published in the UK in 2014 by
New Environment Books
8 Somerset St, Bristol BS2 8NB, UK

British Library Cataloguing in Publication Data
A catalogue record for this book is available
from the British Library

ISBN 978-0-9928789-0-0

© **Roderick Leslie 2014**
Text (unless otherwise attributed)

The right of Roderick Leslie to be identified as the author of this work has been asserted by him in accordance with the Copyright, Designs and Patents Act 1988.

Editor: Jill Rowe
Typesetting: Anna Udagawa
Cover design: Richard Baggot-Lavelle

All rights reserved. Apart from the quotation of brief passages in reviews no part of this book may be reproduced in any form without permission from the publisher and copyright owner.

Printed in Poland by Books Factory (booksfactory.eu)

Further copies of this book may be obtained from:
R Leslie, 8 Somerset Street, Bristol BS2 8NB
for £12.99 + £2.50 p&p (UK only).
Cheque made payable to R Leslie.

For other information and overseas postage rates
please email: rodleslie@btinternet.com.

Contents

Forests in Crisis	5
Towards the 'Flow Country'	9
The New Forestry	30
Recreation	49
Habitat	69
Privatisation 1: 1993-4	92
Land and Timber	94
The New Forest	107
Organisation and Management	122
The Cutting Edge	134
Privatisation 2: 2010-11	165
Future Forests	174
Glossary	203
Index	210

Acknowledgements

First, thanks to all my Forestry Commission colleagues over the years, many named in the book, all greatly valued. Everything I write about was a team effort and the credit belongs to everyone involved.

Thanks to Jonathon Porritt for reading an early draft. Special thanks to my wife Jill for editing but, more importantly, for the support she has given me through the long process of bringing this book to publication. Thank you to Anna Udagawa who typeset and brought the book to production readiness, Bryn Thomas of Trailblazer Publications for production advice and to Richard Baggot-Lavelle for the cover design.

Author Biography

I knew I wanted to manage land by the time I finished my degree in Agricultural and Forest Sciences at Keble College, Oxford. Joining the Forestry Commission was fortuitous, a job advert in a Sunday paper during my final year, and 30 years later I found myself in charge of the largest land holding in a single ownership in England, the 600,000 magnificent acres of the Forestry Commission's nationally owned forests.

I joined as a trainee in Northumberland, moving on a year later to North Yorkshire, working in field management – timber harvesting, restocking, recreation, conservation and forest planning – for six years before moving to Work Study in East Anglia. Based in Thetford Forest I was responsible for developing timber-harvesting systems, introducing new machinery including one of the first complete harvesting machines in Britain, and for chemical application systems. Three years later I was moved at short notice to become National Wildlife and Conservation Officer in the FC's Edinburgh HQ and was immediately plunged into the biggest crisis the FC had ever faced, the Flow Country dispute in the far north of Scotland. My personal interest in birds and nature conservation became crucial not just to the Flow Country, but also developing FC's new conservation strategy. Moving to England in 1988, I worked with private woodland owners and developing environmental policy and delivery, initially for one-third of England, then half and finally the whole country.

After a short spell as Chief Executive of Forest Enterprise England (the land management arm of FC), my last job was Head of Policy, where I led the development of a new forest strategy for England and, perhaps most importantly, the government's strategy for woodfuel which is revolutionising the economics of forestry in lowland England. Leaving the FC, I had hoped for some peace but quickly got drawn into the campaign against the government's attempt to sell all the Forestry Commission forests. My rather rarefied skills in national forest policy were suddenly in demand and I have worked as a consultant for the Institute of Chartered Foresters, the economic consultancy Eftec and for the Forestry Commission, as well as writing for the forestry press, in particular the leading industry magazine, *Forestry Journal*.

Roderick Leslie

Chapter 1

Forests in Crisis

Early in 2011 the Government published its proposals to sell all 637,000 acres of Forestry Commission (FC) managed, nationally owned forests. 550,000 people signed the 38 Degrees petition against the sale. 100 well-known names ranging from the Archbishop of Canterbury to Dame Judi Dench wrote to *The Times* in protest. Prime Minister David Cameron's dramatic U-turn just weeks later has come to symbolise the failure to think through dogma-driven beliefs to practical delivery. The issue penetrated to the core of the coalition government's agenda: real 'big society' on the loose versus the controlled government-friendly version David Cameron tried to sell. What remains extraordinary is how this third-order political issue grew to lose a Secretary of State and her supporting Minister their jobs and is still rumbling on today.

Forestry Commission forests are owned by the Nation and in all three countries the Forestry Commission is the largest single manager of land. In England that is 258,000 hectares (637,000 acres) including the New Forest, Forest of Dean, Kielder, Dalby and Grizedale forests. Ownership is vested in the Secretary of State for Environment, Food and Rural Affairs. About one-third of the estate is leasehold, some with 'forestry purposes only restrictions', which often limits public access. Some forests have other rights to graze animals or mine coal and there are extensive areas of habitat that are not forest, including the largest-surviving lowland heath in northwest Europe, a massive 14,000 hectares of the New Forest. All the freehold land is dedicated for public access on foot under the-

Countryside and Rights of Way Act 2000 (CRoW), and the whole estate is certified under the UK Woodland Assurance Scheme (UKWAS) and by the international Forestry Stewardship Council (FSC). Many of the forests are new, planted since 1919 to form a strategic supply of timber in time of war, but many English forests also have long histories, including forests in Crown ownership before the formation of the Forestry Commission. Forestry Commission forests are just 18% of England's 1.1 million hectares of woodland and 2% of the whole of England. Over the last 50 years they have become synonymous with open access and a warm welcome: the place where nervous countryside users can be sure they won't be shouted at by irate landowners. These are the 'National Forests' of England that the debate is all about.

And there has been a vast amount of debate in the media, in parliament and amongst individual citizens. In the parliamentary debate before the U-turn, speeches by constituency MPs from all sides of the House of Commons were outstanding in both their passion and accuracy: these were people who had listened, learnt and understood. The government was less well informed and stumbled into mistake after mistake. Debate in both the media and public arenas was variable, ranging from the well informed to the wildly inaccurate. Very few commentators got the whole story. In particular, the advocates for selling the forests assumed throughout that this was just about timber and therefore just about a bit of land to be traded as a simple commodity. Land and conservation NGOs circled the spoils like vultures, inspiring the Prime Minister to state that he believed the National Trust and Woodland Trust would manage the 'Heritage' forests better than the Forestry Commission. A view they seemed happy to go along with until Jonathon Porritt launched a swingeing attack on both their positions, which were way out of line with public opinion, and competence.

But in the whole debate one voice has been completely silent: the voice of the people who actually run the national forests, the Forestry Commission. It is well known now that that voice was

Chapter 1: Forests in Crisis

silent within government too – assuming the Forestry Commission would be against its plans, the government did not consult it. It led to a string of elementary errors as Defra (Department for Environment, Food and Rural Affairs) civil servants, used to relying on the FC for advice, struggled with an unfamiliar field of work.

A confused picture ranged from violent criticism of FC conifer planting, often dating back 30 or 40 years and some not even relating to England, to fierce support from the local users who live close to, and visit, the forests on a day-to-day basis.

FC's silence may have led to the assumption that it has had little effect on what has happened. The reality is very different and that is the story I want to tell – how the FC changed from a public pariah after the 'Flow Country' (see Chapter 2) debacle in the late 1980s to a liked and trusted organisation with many supporters and admirers today. It got there by following many of the principles the Prime Minister advocated: recognition that it had to get close to the people who use and love the Nation's forests, listen to what they wanted and even change the way it managed. Not easy to accept for a traditional, rather retiring, Government body.

There was real direction, real vision in what the FC set out to do and, as recent events show, it probably succeeded more than anyone could have expected.

I was lucky enough to be at the heart of many of the events that shaped how the FC is today. I was Wildlife & Conservation officer at FC headquarters in Edinburgh during the 'Flow Country', moving to England as Environment Manager for one-third of the country, later the whole of England, and then Chief Executive of Forest Enterprise England, the agency that manages the forests, and finally Head of Policy for England, working closely with Defra. The story of what the FC did is the missing link in the debate about the future of the National Forests.

This is a personal memoir, not a comprehensive history. It is how I saw things and there will be many other views. I hope that what it lacks is made up for by what is often missing from histories:

what people were actually thinking and why they did things. This is particularly important for the FC because the written record is just about as opaque as it possibly could be: reading an FC annual report tells you a bit about what is going on, although frequently cutting-edge developments are missed, but nothing about the philosophy and direction of the organisation. That has been even more the case since devolution from the late 1990s, with three distinct country approaches.

Foresters don't help. Retiring by nature and conservative with a small 'c', they work on a different timescale to most people: they talk seriously about 400-year lives for broadleaved trees, and work with timber from trees planted before Victoria came to the throne. Foresters are a minority within a tiny minority – people who make their living from the countryside – in an overwhelmingly urban society. They are very good at getting things done: the practical achievement of afforestation is not in doubt, even if the wisdom of some of the planting is.

The ability of foresters to change and adapt faced with new challenges has been proved by the Forestry Commission story – in particular, they have been surprisingly successful in working with others: partners, local communities, and building trust and confidence. I think that's probably because in a world of spin and extravagant promises there's a level of honesty rare in the modern world. When others bid high and settle for less, foresters expect to deliver what they've committed to – whether it is planting one million hectares of new forests or restoring 35,000 hectares of ancient woodland.

It leaves foresters and the Forestry Commission in a peculiar position in the modern world, at one level rather naive, at another strong because they come across as a beacon of reliability in a shifting, superficial world.

Chapter 2

Towards the 'Flow Country'

The Forestry Commission I joined in 1976 was at a turning point. I started in Northumberland where the last big upland planting in England was underway at Uswayford just below the Cheviot. As a trainee I planted broadleaves along the burn – planting conifers right up to stream sides had stopped by 1976: visiting 10 years later I found trespassing sheep had eaten the lot! Up to the 1970s the FC was completely dominated by new planting.

The Commission's story from 1919 is extraordinary: from the base of a tiny number of trial conifer plantings it went on to deliver the UK's largest-ever planned land-use change. For the first 50 years an explosive mix of practical research, combined with exceptional delivery skills, ingenuity and imagination, drove planting forward. In the days before widespread car ownership, the uplands where the Commission worked were very remote and very poor – even into the 1970s when I joined there were remnants of the real poverty and hard grind the planters faced.

As most people know, the Commission was set up to provide a home-grown timber supply for the coal mines in case imports were cut off by war, as they were by the German U-boat campaign in 1917. The early Commission was, however, less single minded than it's been portrayed – alongside the forests, better land was kept for smallholdings for its workers. From the very beginning, as economic depression struck, employment became a key objective. It was central to the planting of the poor, sandy Brecks – Thetford Forest – on the Suffolk/Norfolk border, and the Prince of Wales's

Duchy of Cornwall planted the Dartmoor forests (which later came to the FC) for the same reason. Limited technology combined with a strong forestry ethos led to varied and attractive plantings based on soil quality, so there was a lot of larch alongside Douglas Fir and spruce. Large areas of broadleaves were planted on the best soils, frequently in mixtures, later neglected so the conifers won out, suppressing most of the broadleaves. The early FC's main financial pressure was annual budgets – often cut in those hard times – but it had neither the technology nor economic imperative to plant every square inch.

Trees grow so slowly that the FC had to take chances based on the performance of young trees from those early trials. What trees to plant was critical and it took bold decisions: going for conifers was easy, they grew straight and fast and on poorer soils than broadleaves. The speed trees grow at is measured by 'yield class': this is the highest annual increment of timber achieved during the life of the crop, usually peaking in the latter part of the rotation – trees are felled well before biological maturity because after a point in the midlife of the stand growth continues, but at a slower rate. Broadleaves average a yield class of 4-6, Scots Pine 8-12 and Sitka Spruce and Douglas Fir 12-18. Timber value goes up faster than yield class, because the faster trees grow the more of their volume is bigger timber that can be used for sawn timber (planks and beams).

Only Scots Pine is native to Britain because other common European species didn't make it here before Britain became an island. Norway Spruce was the most obvious of these so was a clear early choice alongside Scots Pine. However, trees from all over the world were tested and it was species from North West America that came out top, particularly suited to the UK's similar oceanic climate. Douglas Fir had been planted as a specimen tree from its introduction in the early 1800s so, like Redwoods, it was known that it could grow to a great size and it featured heavily in early plantings on better soils and has produced fine timber. Of all the

Chapter 2: Towards the 'Flow Country'

conifers, well-thinned Douglas Fir produces the biggest trees – it will pile volume onto fewer stems, whilst Sitka Spruce spreads weight more evenly across the stand. What this means is that yield class for yield class Douglas has a higher percentage in the top-value saw-log category.

Sitka Spruce isn't actually that widespread in its native range – Douglas Fir and the Redwoods cover far more of North America's west coast. However, it was the species increasingly favoured in the western uplands and it was an inspired choice. Its biggest problem in the UK is that it has been too successful – allied to the design (or lack) of the forests it was planted with. A lot of rubbish has been talked about Sitka: this is after all the legendary wood from which wartime Mosquito bombers were built. As a specimen tree it is very beautiful, tall and majestic with sweeping branches, the silvery underside of the needles shining in bright sunlight. Its wood is valued for paper-making because of its 'brightness' and therefore lower need for costly and polluting bleaches. Most of the larger (saw-log) Sitka timber now goes into graded construction timber, the market foresters were aiming for once the priority changed from mining timber. Its prickliness, one of the many factors that don't endear it to countryside lovers, made it least palatable to deer – and it's a tough tree, its needles protected by a thick waxy layer.

But even Sitka had its limits and that's where Lodgepole Pine, also from western North America, came in. Through root adaptation Lodgepole can survive waterlogging. It can even dry out ground as a pioneer species. That's where the good news ends: Lodgepole has been a pretty unmitigated disaster for forestry. There is huge variation between different geographic origins – provenances – and thousands of hectares were planted with varieties that simply turned into bushes or grew better, but with an elegant curved sweep to the lower stem – the very bit that needs to be straight for saw timber. Its timber proved to be inferior – a bull put into a field newly fenced with Lodgepole stakes went round leaning on one after another, snapping every one. However, probably worst of all, it allowed forestry to push its way into places that with hindsight should best have been left alone, in particular in the 'Flow Country' of the far north of Scotland.

The memory of the planting of these early forests is fading fast. What were they like? It is hard to imagine the wide horizons of the newly planted forest nearly 100 years on. As land was bought into the 'plantable reserve' it would invariably have been heavily grazed upland grass or heather. The areas involved were huge and whole forests were sometimes planted in just a few years. There were planting targets to meet and literally hundreds of men were put to work planting.

In the early days turves were cut by hand, turned over to give a raised planting position (to stop roots getting waterlogged) and a weed-free planting site. Later, ploughs took over. Furrows stretched up hill and down dale across the moorlands, with regular cut-off drains. Cut-offs stopped furrows washing out and huge quantities of silt rushing downstream. Newly ploughed and planted sites were geometric: regular brown lines on a pale yellow landscape.

For the first few years the trees are invisible. They start slowly but as their branches join – canopy closure – growth accelerates and the landscape starts to change, significantly from the outside, totally on the inside, as long views are replaced by a wall of trees. Fire was the biggest threat to the young planting: not, as most people assume, in the heat of summer. The highest risk was early spring, dry winds blowing through the previous year's dead, tinder-dry grass. Fire could sweep through huge areas of young trees faster than a man could run, so constant vigilance was essential and a badly managed fire could ruin a forester's career. Other hazards included vole plagues. Barn Owls, Kestrels and Long Eared Owls nested in and around abandoned shielings and fed on this feast resulting from the removal of sheep grazing. Hen Harriers and Short Eared Owls joined the bonanza, nesting on the ground amongst the trees. Vigorously persecuted by Grouse-keepers, the departure of the men for the First World War allowed Harriers to spread from Orkney

Chapter 2: Towards the 'Flow Country'

back to mainland Britain. They followed the forestry planting south through Scotland and into Wales, but as the safe new habitat disappeared with the growth of the trees they retreated; in England persecution has reduced them to extinction as a breeding bird.

Young trees were grown in local nurseries for each forest. Often women weeded the beds and transplanted the hundreds of thousands of seedlings. Lifted – dug up – with bare roots, the trees were transported to the hills, kept 'heeled in' in temporary beds until the planters collected them in their canvas shoulder bags and planted them with a spade – often a simple garden spade, although on peat soils in Northumberland an ingenious semi-circular spade produced a plug of soil under which the trees roots were neatly popped. On good, regular ploughing a man could plant over 1,000 trees a day, barely breaking step to dig the slot, pop in the tree roots and firm the tree in place with his passing heel.

In the uplands trees were planted in the spring, just before they spring into life from winter dormancy. In places as high as Uswayford it was a race between the snow clearing and the trees flushing, producing their new spring needles. A brutally tough job, the early workers were hired and fired virtually by the day, but it was welcome work in communities with few opportunities for cash earnings. The economics of farming the hills was marginal. FC had compulsory purchase powers; it only tried to use them once, in Wales, and was rightly seen off very sharply. However, the judgement that the area was marginal for farming was confirmed as 80% of the area went over to forestry through free market sales over the next 20 years.

Rather than a dispossession, forestry was a buyer of last resort for hill farmers who had little or nothing to look forward to. In remote upland communities forestry was generally welcomed as a positive development, bringing in wages and keeping people in jobs and on the land.

By the 1970s economic objectives had replaced the original strategic aims and this had a profound effect on how the FC planted: pressure was on to maximise output from the land, which meant planting as much of the forest area as possible.

It resulted in two equally damaging practices: in some of the earlier forests when space for planting ran out foresters used the new technology to go back and plant areas such as bogs that had been impossible first time round.

In England the plantable reserve was very small and in my early days in Yorkshire I oversaw the planting of the last fragment, a bog called May Moss, and FC has spent the last decade looking for funding to remove the trees to restore it to bog.

In the lowlands the new economics led to extensive conifer planting in existing broadleaved woodland. The logic was taken to an extreme in eastern England where young Oak plantations were poisoned, because theory said that even with a 20-year start conifers would produce more timber quicker. Even at that time many foresters questioned the logic of what seemed like sacrilege, killing good healthy trees.

Conifers had been planted in broadleaved woods for a long time. In 1979 I prepared a plan for the coniferisation of a wood at Falling Fosse in the North Yorks Moors which I'm glad to say was never implemented. Initially, when labour was abundant, all the broadleaves were felled but that was expensive and by the time I arrived in Yorkshire shade bearers like Western Red Cedar, a second choice for British forestry, were being underplanted under untouched broadleaved woodland. It worked badly, with poor survival, and when Sandy Calder, a very experienced forester, took over as District Officer he stopped it immediately.

How well conifers fared depended on the soil. On brown earths and light, acid podzols in the west exceptional Douglas Fir grew. On heavier soils – such as those in Northamptonshire where most Oak trees were killed – it was generally disastrous: broadleaves fought back and conifers struggled. It took immense effort and large quantities of the notorious herbicide 2-4-5T to get stands away and even then pines rocked in clays waterlogged in

Chapter 2: Towards the 'Flow Country'

winter and cracked open in summer. Finally, in the 1990s, the stress of this extreme regime prematurely killed much of the Norway Spruce that had been planted.

As ever, the evidence of what forestry had done remained all too visible and I will come back to it in discussing ancient woodland. However, what has disappeared almost completely from the landscape and from memory are the many ancient woods cleared for agriculture between 1945 and 1985. I personally inspected woods in North Yorkshire for felling licences to remove them for agriculture in the early '80s. The most famous, now the exemplar coppice woodland, is Suffolk Wildlife Trust's Bradfield Woods, which was only saved from destruction when a sapling lashed back and tragically killed the bulldozer operator.

One further species, Corsican Pine, played a key part: it was much faster-growing than Scots and became the species of choice on sandy soils in southern England. It is rarer further north because, away from the coast, it is affected by the disease Brunchorstia which causes die back from the top: by the North York Moors, which had a lot of sandy plateau soils, Corsican Pine sickened when planted more than about 15 miles from the coast, whereas it thrived in the heart of East Anglia and became the staple tree species for the 20,000-hectare (ha) Thetford Forest.

As the world slumped into the nuclear age the strategic rationale for forestry looked increasingly shaky – future war was going to be short and brutal, no long siege. So what were the forests for? For foresters, planting trees – re-forestation – was an end in itself: but how to impress a sceptical Treasury? The answer was economic: home-grown timber as a business. With it came new concepts of planning and economics – in particular Net Discounted Revenue (NDR) to predict future returns – often over 50 years away, the economic justification needed to finance the continuing planting programme. It resulted in a big shift from the pre-war way of doing things. Forestry was at a crossroads: it could have gone down the route of a multi-functional landuse, based on ecological restoration through re-forestation. The famous ecologist Frank Fraser-Darling, author of the West Highland Survey, promoted this point of view and as a result ended up doing most of his best-known work in the USA, not the UK. But this was an age of single purpose, driven by the white heat of technology. Forest policy mirrored agricultural policy, an all-out drive for the production of a single, hard commodity: timber.

There is no doubt foresters played their part – but the modern belief that it was entirely their fault is simply wrong. What happened reflected both the spirit of the times and a wider political drive. Economics and technology came together in a toxic mix: both the will and the ability to plant more and more land were there. Powerful ploughs ironed out the variations in the land and in the rolling hills of Dumfries and Galloway stopped at nothing – conifers were planted right up to the edges of burns. As the quality of the land got poorer, phosphate fertiliser enabled trees to grow on infertile soils and hardy Sitka Spruce became the default species – the land was way beyond trees such as Douglas Fir.

As I will explain, forestry has changed. We should perhaps be more concerned today that to a large extent agriculture hasn't; and for people at the cutting edge in the Forestry Commission, it is a huge frustration that it is so difficult to get across the message that land can provide more than one benefit at a time.

One vital, and tragic, lesson from all this was that the last 10% – the pure Lodgepole, the conifers in clay ancient woods – did the most damage for the least return. The first thing I have always looked for in forest planning is: where is the timber value? Often less than 50% produces more than 80% of the value. In cases like the Dorset Heaths, described later, there were significant areas of planted pine that were clearly never going to grow valuable timber but were still having a serious impact on the site's heathland ecology. Time and again it became clear that we were arguing over stands that weren't that valuable. It is a lesson forestry is well on the way to learning. I am not so sure about the wider countryside

Chapter 2: Towards the 'Flow Country'

where the same sort of religious zeal is applied to agricultural systems: in some cases the best bet might be to back off, reduce intensity and look towards delivering a wider range of benefits than just food.

There had been criticism from very early in the Commission's planting, most notably in the Lake District in the 1930s. Most of the early opposition to planting was on landscape grounds and frequently justified: it wasn't just the sudden change, but the way that change played out: stark, straight edges against legal boundaries, whole hillsides darkened by solid single-species planting, landscape and historic features submerged beneath a sea of trees, fishing and footpaths lost. However, it was nature conservation that brought an end to upland planting in the late 1980s. Conservation impacts were recognised, though recorded with a degree of regret, but there was also fatalism that this change was preordained and unquestionable. The Nature Conservancy Council (NCC, later English Nature now Natural England) had long held reservations about upland planting but its only real tool against politically supported agriculture and forestry was the SSSI's (Site of Special Scientific Interest) system, and its application had to be limited to the best sites because there simply wasn't the political support for very large areas. Even then, NCC faced problems in the uplands over the question of 'what is so different that side of the fence to make it designated but the other side not?'

But the FC I joined wasn't about planting – it was the tipping point of the big transition from planting to felling. In North Yorkshire, where I worked from 1977 to 1982, felling was well underway, with some of the earliest Douglas Fir in Dalby Forest already being clear felled. These were stunning trees – frequently averaging over one cubic metre/stem and stretching the Ford County tractors skidding them out – dragging them behind the tractor – to the limit. They had been well thinned and produced premium timber. Having got at last to the point of exploiting what they'd set out to grow, foresters were strangely reluctant to get on with the job – early thinning was erratic and unsystematic: often good close to the forest office and neglected in the remoter corners. From 1978 we set out to thin the North Yorks Moors from end to end. The key forestry benefit of thinning is that the remaining stems grow thicker quicker – and the whole aim of conifer silviculture is to maximise the larger wood that can be sawn – as opposed to smaller wood used for paper pulp, chipboard, MDF and fencing. It also makes woods lighter and more attractive. In woods planted on farmland with identical ground flora, conifers and broadleaves diverge as the canopy closes and conifers shade out more plants but after 80-90 years well-thinned stands of conifer and broadleaves have similar ground floras.

Thinning has, however, been an Achilles heel of British forestry – with the exception of a tiny minority of private estates, under-thinning has been endemic. It's possible that over the first conifer rotation it has actually cost forestry more than all the highly publicised environmental costs put together.

The Yorkshire forests were a mixture of pine, larch, Douglas Fir, spruce and broadleaves, mainly Beech but also extensive Alder woods along the becks. Sitka Spruce was much less dominant than in most big FC forests because the rich soils allowed species like Douglas to be grown and the east coast rainfall was marginal for Sitka. With outcropping limestone, the forests have an unusually rich ecology. The uplands, their sheep walks and forests, are generally acidic. There were two main products from thinning: in Yorkshire then untreated larch was popular with local farmers for fencing and sold well, and both pine and larch went into pit-wood (props for the coal mines) which, despite the change in FC objectives, remained a very lively market right up to the miners' strike.

Mining timber was produced in the forest by standing sales merchants who bought the trees on the hoof, felled and processed them. Conifer mining timber was in the round, the bark peeled in England (some Welsh mines used unpeeled timber) and produced in a bewildering range of very precise sizes. These reflected different technical needs, but also differing custom & practice between

Chapter 2: Towards the 'Flow Country'

mining areas and even individual pits. It was worth the complexity because prices were high.

Both thinning and the age of final felling are determined by management tables calculated from regularly measured sample plots. Trees start slowly, growth accelerates and runs at a high level before dropping off well before biological maturity – the point where growth plateaus, stops, and the tree then goes into decline and finally dies. The point of felling, where both timber and money are maximised over several rotations, is generally after growth starts to fall off but well before it stops and the tree starts to decline. For Douglas Fir and Sitka Spruce this is usually between 50 and 60 years, a little longer for pine, a little less for larch. Either side of the optimum date you start to lose money; not much 5 years either way, but more significantly the earlier felling is than the optimum. Delaying felling also losses money, but less so than early felling.

Still focussed on the triumphs of the planting phase, foresters were caught out by two unexpected problems as the forests matured. The first was wind: in the more exposed uplands, with wetter soil, trees started to blow over well before they reached theoretical maturity. Disrupting the tight canopy by thinning could bring on wind-blow very early, and in the most vulnerable areas thinning had to be abandoned completely. This was not the 'catastrophic' damage of a 1987 style hurricane but 'endemic' windthrow, creeping damage caused by normal winter gales, toppling trees quite reliably as they reached what came to be called 'terminal height'. Harwood Forest in Northumberland is a big regular trapezium shape on a west–east axis. Blow started on the exposed west face and it was cleared up. Then the next bit blew and about 10 years later the felling, chasing blow all the time, popped out at the far, eastern, end. Wind remains a dominant factor in upland forest planning. It had its impact in Yorkshire too, despite a much-lower hazard due to dryer soils and lower elevation. Many of the senior foresters had been through the early wind-blow in Kielder and were terrified the same thing would happen – it took some persuasion to get them thinning and even Yorkshire wasn't invulnerable – a big hole caused by an out-of-control standings sale contractor proved the point by starting a wind-blow focus which spread and spread.

The other problem was replanting after felling – known as re-stocking. FC by now knew everything there was to know about planting trees. Restocking would be easy. Kielder was one of the earliest large upland forests with major clear-felling. When I joined in 1976 the whole of North East Conservancy was beating up (re-placing lost trees) at over 100% on restocks: for every tree planted at least one more had to be planted to replace it because so many of the initial re-planting had died. Ploughing, which foresters had come to rely on, wasn't possible on stump-strewn clear-fells. Soil water levels – relieved in new planting by ploughing and draining – shot up after felling, and planting trees at a regular 2-metre interval could leave them sitting in a pool of water in winter, and dying as a result. Restocks also had two damaging pests, the bark beetles *Hylobius* and *Hylastes* both of which lived in the wood debris after felling, and gnawed the fragile bark of the tiny young trees. It is against these pests that virtually the only significant insecticide use in forestry has been deployed.

Finally, the way trees were grown and looked after had got lax. Paul Tabbush's research showed that even throwing plastic bags of trees off the back of a lorry could significantly reduce their viability. Trees heated up in the sun, even in low air temperatures, in the 'greenhouse' of a clear plastic bag. FC developed an opaque black bag – but it took Mike Ashmole, of Fountain Forestry, to force them into manufacture and widespread use.

The other big factor was the explosion in deer numbers, Roe in England and Roe, Red and Sika in Scotland, their browsing weakening and even killing trees to the extent that, for a long time, re-stocking in many upland forests could only survive through fencing.

Even in the easier conditions of Yorkshire beating up was running at 40% but more seriously, tree selection had got lazy with a

Chapter 2: Towards the 'Flow Country'

drift from testing, delicate Douglas Fir to easier Sitka Spruce. Sandy Calder and I set out to reverse this: using our local nursery at Wykeham, we arranged for trees to be lifted and delivered on the day of planting – from nursery to forest in less than 24 hours, we waited for the soil to warm up in the spring and finally, rather than reinforcing failure, we beat up with Sitka, not Douglas. We knew mixed stands worked well from the first rotation. Eventually we reintroduced ploughing which solved the weed problem on these rich soils.

With standard ploughs it was essential to get below the root plates, both more drastic and expensive than ideal, but after I moved to the operational research branch (Work Study) in 1982 I was able to trial Swedish scarifiers which used big toothed discs to create the bare patches we were looking for by riding over, not undercutting, the old stumps.

Getting into felling had a number of effects that are easier to see in hindsight. The first rotation, especially the 'dark ages' when whole forests were dense, middle-aged, planted right up to roads and rides, happened only once, and were at their most extreme ever at the point when upland forestry hit the buffers. In a place like Yorkshire, soil and species differences would have broken up the forest even had felling always been on time without restructuring.

Net Discounted Revenue quietly died and was replaced by cash flow. The pressure to plant every square inch declined. Even broadleaves started to get a look in again. I clearly remember incorporating three hectares of broadleaved planting into a 300-ha plan in 1981, as brave then as planting conifers now.

Dalby was already part of Yorkshire life by 1980, a hugely popular recreation destination, with enthusiastic FC foresters putting a lot of effort into welcoming people and explaining forestry. Oil exploration had created a tarmacked road, which became the forest drive. Forest drives were very popular in the early mass car-owning era when driving for a day out in the country became popular. They declined in the 1980s, all except at Dalby which is more popular than ever. Dropping down into the Dalby Valley, visitors found extensive open meadows onto which they could drive their cars, a small visitor centre, and an even-smaller kiosk for ice creams and tea. There were waymarked walks with trail leaflets all along the drive. Half way down the drive the new Staindale Lake had just been completed and the drive ends with a stunning view across the high moors before diving into the remote valleys around Langdale End. Along the route at regular intervals were small car parks and picnic tables.

Even then conifers had entered public consciousness as a 'bad thing' and I learnt an early lesson talking to a couple luxuriating in the sun with the Sunday papers beside their car. Were they having a nice time? O, yes, wonderful, wasn't it beautiful? And what did they think of conifers? No, they didn't like them at all. Where they sat they were completely surrounded by larch, Douglas Fir, a few Sitka Spruce and some Scots Pine. Only the stream was lined with broadleaves. I've still to meet anyone who isn't impressed by a really fine stand of big Douglas Fir. But that's not an attempted apologia: even I, as a hardened forester, can see why people hated the huge, functional new forests – and in this era you really could drive (or, far worse, walk) literally for 10 miles or more through many big forests of absolutely solid, impenetrable thicket-stage Sitka Spruce, the only views out down the geometric management rides to.... more Sitka Spruce.

Although the FC was – and is – a very disciplined organisation, there were significant differences in approach. The west of England did not implement the attack on broadleaves with anything like the ferocity of the east. Morley Pennistan developed a more sensitive approach, slipping in conifers in small groups and as far as I know there was no poisoning of growing trees. Thanks to Jack Chard and Bill Grant, North West England became leaders in both conservation and recreation, Grizedale becoming particularly famous for its tarns, deer management and early art in the forest projects.

Chapter 2: Towards the 'Flow Country'

Most foresters had an interest in wildlife and they to an extent recognised the penalties of what they were doing but saw them as inevitable, almost an act of God, impossible to influence. There was certainly a macho element where the environmentally sensitive were seen as inferior to the hard operations foresters, ploughing and felling all before them. This was not an attitude always born out by results on the ground, where the best managers were often best across the board.

Foresters were severely programmed to plant and plant everything they could. A fascinating area of conflict was deer lawns (open areas selected by wildlife rangers to attract deer and facilitate shooting to control populations and therefore damage to trees). You would have thought foresters would have latched onto this and realised that leaving this space would more than pay them back later in reduced loss of trees and costly beating up – not a bit of it, planters would cheerfully plant space marked clearly as 'open'. It probably reflected the lowly status of wildlife rangers in the FC pecking order.

Whilst FC generally led forestry thinking it was an FC-trained ranger, Ronnie Rose, who left and joined the Economic Forestry Group (EFG), who advanced new planting design in the 1970s. Ronnie did a great job in Eskdalemuir – and Ronnie, a born communicator, and EFG an effective private company, publicised their achievement in a way FC would have struggled to do. Here were the deer glades and trees kept back from streamsides, attractive lakes and a forest that felt less industrial. Broadleaves were yet to come. Bearing in mind that EFG were selling forestry investment to private clients I suspect that every hectare unplanted repaid them threefold, because the forest was so much more attractive, and in the early days of environmental consciousness they had an impressive story to tell.

Ronnie's work covered the whole of the EFG Eskdalemuir Forest and was, though wildlife led, quite holistic in its approach to the forest environment. The one thing it did not fully cover was landscape and an otherwise excellent design was let down by a practice unique to EFG of leaving a row unplanted at regular intervals, creating garish contrasting lines on these white grass hills. FC's first national move on the environment had in fact been on landscape, through the appointment of Dame Sylvia Crowe as consultant landscape architect. A powerful and imaginative character, she became something of an institution in FC, famous for having foresters dashing round the forest with helium balloons to allow her to chart the landscape against the map on the ground, far less easy to do than you might think.

Dame Sylvia had a huge impact. She pointed out that the landscape had to be viewed and planned from eye-level viewpoints, not on a flat map. Her skilful landscape designs banished straight lines forever. The other invaluable lesson she taught was scale: if the landscape is big you've got to do it big. This went against a general conservationist view that smaller was also better which had become the norm in the even bigger landscapes managed by the US Forest Service, and had left hillsides looking as if they had caught measles, with lots of small felling coupes. Dame Sylvia was followed by FC foresters, led by Duncan Campbell and Oliver Lucas, who retrained as landscape architects.

In the north, however, the storm clouds were gathering. The NCC, led by Chief Scientist Derek Ratcliffe, had become increasingly desperate as they saw forestry eating up more and more of the uplands with no end in sight. The Royal Society for the Protection of Birds (RSPB) were alongside them fighting and losing a battle in the Berwyns in Wales. NCC tried to publish a critique of forestry in 1979 but the forestry lobby managed to block it. It was a big mistake: by the time it came back in 1986 attitudes in conservation had hardened and NCC's views were far more critical and damming.

A contributory factor was the FC's Wood Production Outlook, promoting the case for more afforestation, which passed off conservation concerns with a bland statement that woods were really

Chapter 2: Towards the 'Flow Country'

rather good for wildlife, completely ignoring the case for the wildlife of the open uplands. The dispute over Creag Meagaidh in the Scottish Highlands showed that even designated SSSIs were not safe. It was the prelude, however, to a far bigger battle which would change not just the face of British forestry, but also the relative power between conservation and other land uses for ever. The battle was over what came to be famous as the 'Flow Country' – a vast area of low-lying bogs and pools in the very far north of Scotland.

The 'Flow Country' name was actually coined as part of the massive clash that developed between forestry and conservation in the far north of Scotland. Located mainly in Caithness, mainland Britain's northernmost county, the Flow Country is an enormous low-lying area of raised deep peat bogs with clusters of small pools on the top of their shallow domes. The raised bogs roll away, each a gentle dome, fringed by the hills and mountains in the far distance, high to the west, lower to the north and south and flat towards the east coast. Pool systems glitter in the sun (we're there on one of the rare bright days!). Close up, pools sprout bog bean from their dark, peaty waters. Surprisingly, these pools are at the high point of the raised bog, held there by the saturated peat. It's a nerve-racking business walking across the dome of the bog – not for nothing is this called a quaking bog! The air is full of the plaintive piping of Golden Plover, watching their nests or young from behind a clump of heather. If you're lucky you might be bombed by an elegant Arctic Skua.

It is, in fact, the exceptional area in Britain for moorland birds. The combination of the vast complex of bog pools and lochs and its northerly location means it holds a wider range of species than any other part of mainland UK. In addition to the iconic Greenshank, Golden Plover and Dunlin it also has most of the mainland's Arctic Skuas and all the Common Scoter. There are Hen Harriers and Short Eared Owls and very occasionally northern rarities such as Wood Sandpiper. This wealth of birds can be hard to explain because it is exceptionally infertile land and everything is at very low densities.

Forest Vision

Myth and reality are two different countries in this dispute. Forestry did not directly challenge conservation interests (in contrast to Creag Meagaidh which was already an SSSI). The reason forestry was there, and forestry's big concern, was landuse. The Department of Agriculture for Scotland (DAFS) had to clear FC grant aid for forestry planting. It had criteria for what constituted a 'viable' sheep farm and wouldn't release land that it considered part of a 'viable' unit. By the 1980s DAFS' protectionist view was way out of line with real values: it was protecting, through regulation, land which was not remotely viable economically for sheep. The restriction eventually led to a celebrated case where a landowner and serving non-executive Forestry Commissioner planted an area without grant – and without DAFS clearance. The disparity between land values for sheep farming and forestry had got so big that he reckoned he'd make money even without a grant. This inevitably put the cat amongst the pigeons and after a Government flurry it emerged that this would not be repeated. The one area even DAFS extremists weren't defending was the Flow Country so that's where FC, and on a much larger scale, Fountain Forestry, went. To FC and forestry planters it was this land use dispute that filled their horizons: conservation issues barely registered.

The Commissioner may have planted without a grant but he'd still get his tax relief, probably far more valuable and the big driver behind private forestry at the time. This was how Terry Wogan and many other well-known names came to be involved as 'Flow Country' investors, adding another strand to the developing story and a publicity opportunity as juicy as bankers' bonuses today. Tax had risen to 90% under Labour (remember The Beatles' *Taxman*?) and even when it dropped back the lure of getting money back from the Government remained too good to resist.

At the time there was little indication of conservation value – the recently published seminal Nature Conservation Review contained a few limited sites, all justified on their peat lands, and RSPB Scottish Director Frank Hamilton had described it as MAMBA

Chapter 2: Towards the 'Flow Country'

country ('miles and miles of b****r all'). Conservationists hadn't looked hard because, fairly, they hadn't thought anyone would be trying to change this apparently worthless land.

Foresters had to deploy the very best of their technology – particularly the new super-wide apical track shoes that allowed ploughing tractors to virtually walk on water – to plant this land. Experiments showed that mixing Sitka and Lodgepole could work to upgrade production from these poor sites and phosphate fertiliser was essential. All the same, there was sufficient uncertainty about the area's suitability for trees for the Forestry Commissioners to visit to review policy even before the conservation storm broke. Sandy Calder, returning to north Scotland in charge of forest management, immediately put a stop to the planting of pure Lodgepole Pine on the basis it simply wasn't worth the cost. This pulled planting back from the furthest extremes – and ploughing was going right up to the edge of the pool systems, almost impossibly difficult, sodden ground.

I arrived in Edinburgh in spring 1985 as National Wildlife and Conservation Officer, a small cog in FC's rapid upgrading of its environmental capability. I'd warned my new boss, Alastair Rowan, that I felt serious trouble was brewing in the 'Flow Country' when I had first met him a month earlier. He'd been a little dismissive then. An incisive thinker, he wasn't one to leave an issue like that hanging. Almost as soon as I arrived he called me in, told me he'd looked into it, and agreed with my assessment. Led by RSPB, a highly effective campaign developed against forestry in the Flow country. NCC pitched in with it's wider criticism of upland forestry before also focussing on the Flow Country. As the pressure grew so did the understanding of the area's birds and peat land, and the more information there was the worse it got for forestry.

The campaign hit a largely unsuspecting FC and forestry private sector, and the Scottish Office were similarly wrong footed: they didn't have the expertise to judge the factual case and were suspicious of both sides. I spent a lot of time explaining the basic facts – for example, that just because Greenshanks were so sparse didn't mean they weren't as tightly packed as cows in a field – they needed huge territories because the habitat is so poor, and definitely couldn't 'shuffle up' to compensate for habitat lost to forestry. For someone a long way down the pecking order I found myself in some fairly critical situations. Eventually Survival Anglia decided to do a film fronted by the bogman himself, David Bellamy. I was sent to represent the FC and found myself in front of the cameras on a remote hilltop facing some very difficult questions. Finally, David asked whether forestry should have done it and, taking my career in my hands, I replied 'if we'd known what we know now we wouldn't have done'. By that point I was convinced forestry had to withdraw from an unwinnable position: the 'Flow Country' had become a national byword and forestry an environmental pariah.

A complicating factor, one that made life very difficult for NCC in particular, was that in the actual area where the planting was going on, forestry was still seen as a valuable development. Very few people have been to the north coast of Scotland other than John o' Groats. This is an area where mains electricity and telephones were still a bit of a novelty outside the towns of Wick and Thurso. Isolated and poor, paying jobs were at a premium and this land wasn't even worth running sheep on – land prices bottomed at £50/hectare before forestry came on the scene.

What surprises me even more now than then is that the FC did pull back. It was completely against its culture, which was to stand and fight, and the Director General at the time, Gwynn Francis, was a very straight forester who'd made his name reviving Britain's forest-processing sector in the early 1980s. It is all the more to his credit that, no doubt against the advice of many colleagues in both the private sector and FC, he recognised the inevitable and pulled back. It was that which probably took everyone, especially the conservation lobby, by surprise. Certainly the NCC never realised what was happening. They had hit major problems with splits between their England-based scientists driving a hard position and

Chapter 2: Towards the 'Flow Country'

their nervous Scottish colleagues. They'd been seen by the Scottish Office as very partisan in contrast to FC which was probably felt to have given more balanced and helpful advice to bemused civil servants. FC was much stronger in Scotland, to all intents and purposes a rare Scottish-first Government organisation, with a string of Scottish establishment Chairmen to its name.

The crunch came in 1988. The Chancellor announced that the tax concessions that had driven private forestry were to go, in the name of 'tidying up' the tax system. The Government announced that NCC would be split into three country organisations. The day I heard the news my first reaction was 'it should have been us'. FC lived to fight another day by the skin of its teeth – but very badly wounded and facing an uncertain future. Had it stood and fought, as most people expected, it would have been abolished there and then.

The removal of tax concessions brought 'traditional' upland conifer planting to an almost instant halt: it was the money, but also the bad reputation it had gained. Either way, that was it.

I described these events at the time in the book *Birds and Forestry*, co-authored with Mark Avery, and recently republished by Harper Collins.

Chapter 3

The New Forestry

The seeds of FC's survival may well also have been sown in 1985. It was the year David Clark MP, now Lord Clark of Windermere and later FC Chairman through the 2000s, pushed an amendment to the Forestry Act through Parliament. It required the Forestry Commissioners to balance timber production and the environment. It represented a significant change in the FC's remit, was taken very seriously by the Commissioners under Director General George Holme's leadership, and led to immediate changes in policy and practical action to upgrade FC's environmental performance.

This was another crossroads. Everyone accepted something had to be done. There was a significant lobby arguing that conservation should be corralled in just part of the forest – 10% was suggested – so that timber production could go on unconstrained in the rest. This lobby also argued for exiting from conservation obligations, in particular using the forest sales programme to preferentially sell FC-owned SSSIs. The Commissioners took the opposite route and in a crucial, but almost unrecognised, policy statement declared that their view was that the whole forest had conservation value, and that they would not preferentially sell SSSIs. This firmly turned the tide back towards a more holistic approach to forestry.

Two hugely important initiatives were already underway. Forestry had not always treated water well: there is an inherent fault in the ownership of rivers, especially in Scotland, as forestry took the worst land it got the spawning beds, vital but worthless in cash terms. It was downstream owners, farming the better land, that got

Chapter 3: The New Forestry

the fishing. As the intensity of forestry increased, trees were planted right across headwaters, shading out life as spruce closed its dark canopies. There were also serious siltation problems: logically, foresters plumbed their ploughing and drainage straight into the burns. Good practice requires up and down plough furrows to be cut off by drains horizontal to the slope – but it only takes an exceptionally severe rainstorm, or a cut off drain a couple of degrees too steep, for serious erosion to cause a flush of silt, covering gravel spawning beds and, most seriously, making water-supply reservoirs turbid. In one of the most eccentric land-management events I ever encountered, colleagues in Wales were sued by a Chinese laundry: the downstream consequence of a reservoir full of silt.

What tipped the balance, however, was the discovery that forests were acidifying water. The mechanism is that conifer needles collect airborne particles more effectively than grass or heather because they have a far greater surface area. Rain then washes the concentrated pollutants off the trees into watercourses. In much of the acid Welsh and Scottish uplands there is no buffering capacity in the soil – a relatively small acid input can tip the balance severely. Fish and Dippers suffered directly, but the wider implications for the soil and landscape were more serious. I've since wondered to what extent forestry was taken for a ride over acidification: forestry was blamed for 'causing' acidification. This was completely wrong: what forests did was collect pollutants from the air and those pollutants came from coal-fired power stations. How was it that that particular fact was rarely, if ever, mentioned?

Water and acidification became major factors in forestry's still primary obsession in 1985 – finding more land to plant. Intensive discussions led to the first water guidelines, the first in a series which would set the environmental standards for forestry over the next few years. Key measures were much tighter standards for ploughing and draining: the simple expedient of stopping drains well back from watercourses so water could slow, spread, and drop its silt load, keeping conifers well back from watercourses and

Forest Vision

planting more broadleaves. In the most acid-sensitive areas of Wales and south Scotland recently planted conifers were cut back along many miles of watercourses. There were agreements on the maximum level of forestry permitted in acid-sensitive catchments, so as a result there were further restrictions on where new trees could be planted.

The other big change was the broadleaves policy. Led by Sandy Morrison, the Head of Land Use, this was a very major development for forestry, reversing the single-minded focus on conifers of the previous 30 years. The broadleaves policy was sparked largely by the work of two men, Oliver Rackham and George Peterken, whose meticulous ecological and historical research into woodland history completely changed our understanding of native woodlands. Previously, there'd been a rather vague idea about where our remnant woods came from. That native woodland had fallen out of economic use as the demand for the products of traditional 'woodsmanship' declined didn't help: the huge areas coppiced for thatching went out of use as slate and tile came in, as did the demand for firewood as the railways – and coal – reached further and further into the countryside. Britain was so fixed on imported timber that the lodge at Abernethy in the Cairngorms, one of Scotland's largest-surviving native pinewoods and now an RSPB reserve, is built from Scandinavian timber.

The development of the broadleaves policy was hard fought, with RSPB very much in the lead and Ron Davies MP their mouthpiece in parliament. Ron was a master of the parliamentary arts and put down rafts of parliamentary questions to try and trip FC into anomalies – to the extent that the FC Secretary, Peter Clarke, an equally wily operator, ended up with them spread on a large table whilst he and his staff matched and compared them for attempted trips.

The results of this febrile debate were very positive: a vigorous policy favouring broadleaves, stopping forever the total destruction of ancient woodlands through conversion to farmland,

Chapter 3: The New Forestry

and introducing a generous new grant for broadleaved planting. It is a policy that has stood the test of time and all those involved – on both sides of the debate – deserve credit for their achievement.

Not everyone liked it and although I arrived after the policy was launched I played a central role in selling it to often vociferously antagonistic landowners. Probably the fiercest attack was at a Farming & Wildlife Advisory Group (FWAG) meeting where the Chairmen of the county FWAG's – prominent county landowners – laid into me with such abandon that at the end a delegation of their county officers – young professional conservationists – came up to apologise for their Chairmen! I was told time and again it would never work and they all wanted conifers. I learnt an important lesson which hasn't changed one iota in the subsequent years: at the same time landowners were swearing they'd never go along with the scheme, they were filling in their grant forms. The higher grants for broadleaves were, and still are, completely successful in changing behaviour. They've been sold out up to budget (and sometimes well beyond) ever since and barely a conifer was planted on new ground in England by anyone except FC from then on.

One less-positive side effect was the influence the grant rules had on forestry practice: there had to be a minimum limit on how many trees were required to get a full grant. A pragmatic decision was taken that it should be 3 x 3 metres, about 1,100 trees to the hectare. This spacing is far wider than ideal for growing good broadleaved timber but with the high cost of the then new plastic tree shelters (tubes) this spacing matched the grant levels and ensured a closed canopy would develop. By the next decade the 3-metre spacing had acquired a life of its own, almost all but the most discerning and determined owners were planting at 3 metres and most people today believe it is a silviculturally based practice. It's a dangerous example of how a practice put in place for one reason can come to be justified as something quite unrelated.

The threats to broadleaved woodland up to 1985 were seen as so severe that RSPB had bought a significant number of woods in all three countries to protect them. I'm not sure if they have bought any since.

Alastair Scott followed the broadleaves policy with a new policy for Scotland's tiny and important native pinewood resource, again turning years of study and fluctuating FC approaches into hard, clear policy for conservation.

1985 was International Year of the Environment (IYE). John Kennedy, Commissioner for Forest Management, allocated £200,000 to conservation projects. When I arrived in Edinburgh I was told to produce a proposal to spend this money – in two weeks. This funding turned out to be vital: through the projects it paid for, FC were working with the very organisations most opposing the Flow Country – at each other's throats in one area, conservation and forestry were building trust and partnership in others. It was quite a high-wire act but it worked. It also provided funding to partners, with RSPB actually running much of the core research, again building confidence.

I knew and admired Colin Bibby, Head of Research for RSPB, a brilliant and imaginative scientist with the added benefit that he had directed several small projects with FC foresters when he worked on Merlin in Wales. We set up two big projects, one on Nightjar and Woodlark in Thetford Forest and the other on Black Grouse which were getting very rare in north Wales. Both projects represented a shift of emphasis in support of the FC's newly stated policy because they involved the bulk of the forest, not areas set aside for conservation. Both were designed to develop our understanding of management of the forest as a whole.

Nightjar and Woodlark are species of the early stages of replanting and helped develop the understanding of a 'forest cycle', where each stage supports different groups of species. This study showed that these threatened species required a minimum threshold of clearfell size to be able to nest – about 5 hectares for Nightjar – and again went against the prevailing 'small must be better'. At the time the study started, Nightjar were gaining prominence after

Chapter 3: The New Forestry

decades of lack of interest – a common fate for nocturnal species – whilst Woodlark had hardly registered. However, they were at that point probably rarer in the UK than Dartford Warblers, sinking to a low of just 400 pairs. On the surface just a boring little brown bird, Woodlark are actually quite superb. Far less well known than Nightingale, they compete strongly for best British bird song. If Skylark are the 78 vinyl record, a bit thin and scratchy, Woodlark are the CD – the same sort of song, but richer and more rounded and they sing for longer, soaring up above forest clearings until they are lost against the sky, except for the marvellous outpouring of beautiful musical notes. They aren't really a woodland bird. They feed by walking on bare ground amongst clumps of grass, picking off insects. Generally associated with heathland in the UK, they need bare, disturbed, soil and don't do well where there is a continuous cover of grass or heather which rules out most of today's heathland nature reserves, as these tend to be far too far down the sequence of vegetation succession for Woodlark. The shade of a conifer stand before felling, combined with the ground disturbance of the machines extracting timber creates ideal conditions, but for just a few years. That is why a continuous sequence of new felling sites is vital.

Black Grouse were even more interesting because they use both edges and a range of different habitats, for example the nutritious spring ears of bog cotton are very important for feeding the young chicks – assuming the foresters haven't blitzed the bog out of existence. Similarly, birch can be an important food source in the spring and whilst all the feeding is in more open areas, including restocks, the nest site is hidden away in the thicket of the forest. The battle to save Black Grouse in Wales continues, and it is a struggle with FC and RSPB still vigorously engaged – on the same side! There has been a gentle increase in numbers over the years – and it is almost certain the species would be extinct in Wales now without the combined intervention of foresters and conservationists. As part of the programme FC asked for a voluntary ban on shooting Black Grouse in Wales and the shooting community supported it unanimously: no countryman wanted to see this stunning bird lost forever from the Welsh landscape.

What I hadn't realised when I commissioned these research projects was the nature of Government finance: it's very difficult to get anything started but once it's in the budget it takes an act of will to cut it out, so, from one year's official funding, the Thetford project eventually wound up six years later, by which time conservation thinking was firmly embedded. What it led to subsequently was even more surprising and has had a huge impact right up to the present: Nightjar is a 'European' bird, cited in the EU Birds Directive and as numbers grew, Thetford's population crossed the threshold for protection, and almost the whole forest was designated a Special Protection Area (SPA) for birds and an SSSI. Thetford was the second most obvious 'timber' forest after Kielder, and since then non-FC people trying to classify the estate have been taken aback to find the forest is an internationally designated nature conservation site.

The FC had planted a number of large coastal sand dune systems, in some cases to protect houses and farmland from the shifting sands; I also commissioned a research project with the Institute of Terrestrial Ecology (ITE) to do a study on Newborough Forest in Anglesey. What it showed was that without movement lime quickly leached from the sand significantly changing its ecology, particularly dis-favouring some of the rarer dune plants. It was 20 years before this work resurfaced in a continuing debate between the Countryside Council for Wales and FC on one side and local people on the other. Based on the ITE research, conservationists argue that trees need to be removed to allow the dunes to once again move, functioning naturally and protecting rare flora. However, local people are equally concerned about the threat to a surviving Red Squirrel population in the now mature forest.

Alongside these new projects FC's own Research Division had two important and influential research projects underway. Steve Petty's work on birds in Kielder Forest and later in Argyll were

Chapter 3: The New Forestry

adding to the understanding of the changing ecology of the forests. Steve started work on Sparrowhawks as they came into the developing Kielder. As the forest matured Tawny Owls moved in and predated many sitting Sparrowhawks off the nest – so Steve switched his studies to the Tawnies. They had the added advantage that they always used nest boxes when provided (a hole nester by nature, Tawny Owls were found nesting on the ground in these dead-wood free new forests). Steve also followed the rise of Goshawk which established themselves in Kielder during his time. It comes as a shock to most conservationists that predators eat each other and there are frequent calls for control: largely unrecognised in mainstream conservation, forests like Kielder may have reached a point where predator on predator predation actually dominates bird ecology: despite huge areas of vole-rich restocks, Kestrel are the rarest Kielder raptor and Short Eared Owl, common on the first restocks in the 1970s, are very rare, both almost certainly because as they hover or drift gently over the ground concentrating on hunting voles, they are easy targets for Goshawk dashing out from the forest edge.

Working with Colin Bibby when he was in Wales, FC Wildlife Officer Fred Currie had also done very useful work, in particular on the birds of older (retention) stands kept well beyond their felling date and allowed to grow into much bigger trees.

As deer damage soared, Phil Ratcliffe's work on Red Deer was more central to timber management. The deer ate young trees and stripped bark from middle-aged stands. Personally, I think Phil's work was one of the finest pieces of applied population research of the last 30 years and has been hugely underrated probably because he was not a senior academic. Faced with the lore of Red Deer on the open hill – and unable to actually see the forest deer for the trees – he had to start from scratch with new methodology and also an open mind. What he found using a range of methods – vantage point counts, population cohort analysis of deer shot as part of forest management, and a dung count method to assess density – was that there were spectacularly more deer in the forest and they grew faster and better than anyone had imagined. Traditional hill count methods just didn't work (not surprising when you think about it). He held his ground, faced with a barrage of criticism linked to FC cancelling private deer stalking concessions as it tried to bring populations back under control, and won through to a new understanding of forest deer. It wasn't always easy to be taken seriously: explaining dung counts to the august body of the Forestry Commissioners on tour, there was tittering in the back row. Fearlessly Phil turned on them and said 'it may just be shit to you but it's bread and butter to me'.

Key things that came out of Phil's work were the realisation that there was lots of open space – grazing – hidden away in what the foresters liked to think was solid plantation. The other thing was the quality of the habitat: not surprising when you think about it, more sheltered and providing much more food than the open hill. Ideal habitat for deer – and, of course, their natural habitat before man destroyed the forests.

The next group of projects, I have to admit, was a bit of self-indulgence on my part. But it did have a serious side too: a lot of the best forest-planning work is hard to promote because most people don't even notice it, but put up a bird box and everyone recognises conservation is going on. A range of artificial nesting projects had been developed by FC and RSPB, all on a small scale because the money wasn't there to do more. RSPB Highland Officer Roy Dennis had shown how effective artificial eyries for Ospreys could be in boosting the still tiny Scottish population. It got the Ospreys to breed younger because they didn't have to make a new nest, and the man-made nests were more robust than nests made by young, inexperienced Ospreys. However, the big benefit was that the nests could be located where they were difficult to find and raid for eggs. Ospreys are confiding birds – in Florida they nest on pylons next to the freeway – but with the pernicious British egging lust sadly still alive their habit of nesting in easily accessible places was a disaster

Chapter 3: The New Forestry

and a drain on protection resources. So with the IYE money FC put up a whole load more nests tucked well back in the vast forests, miles down forest roads inaccessible to egger's cars, and over the years they really proved their worth, with no robberies at all. They contributed to the increase in Ospreys that has turned them from a rare sight into one of the Highland's most popular spectacles.

Roy had also put up big wooden boxes for Goldeneye Ducks and succeeded in getting them to return as Scottish nesters. But there weren't that many boxes. FC put up hundreds more. As well as boosting the Speyside population I was interested in how far their natural range might extend so we put up boxes through south Scotland into Northern England. The answer, however, was not a lot: the new *Bird Atlas 2007-11*, produced by the British Trust for Ornithology, shows they have spread south – as far as Loch Tay in Perthshire – but no further; it seems fairly clear that this Scandinavian species had come about as far south as it is able to.

Rare Red and Black Throated Divers were in decline in Scotland, failing to produce enough young to keep the population going. They nest beside lochs and suffered from fluctuating water levels flooding their nests and disturbance from people walking the banks. Diver islands made of polystyrene and chicken wire, covered in natural vegetation and moored out in the loch solved both problems but cost money, so again we were able to turn a successful trial into a mainstream programme.

The biggest single tranche of money, £50,000 supporting the broadleaves policy, went to Dalavich Oakwood in Argyll. Again, this project set off much bigger events later. Local staff including Peter Quelch and Alan Stevenson were keen to restore the ancient Oak wood which had been underplanted with Norway Spruce. They were supported by Peter Wormell of the NCC, an inspiring advocate of Scottish native woodland restoration who privately ran his own local provenance tree nursery. It was the classic ancient woodland double whammy: the spruce had grown enough to shade out the ground almost completely, but they couldn't break through an Oak canopy that had closed after the conifer planting. So the ecology was destroyed without actually producing timber. The spruce went, new public access went in, and what eventually turned into the 'Atlantic Oakwoods' EU Life project was born.

The FC had appointed ex-NCC Scottish Director Morton Boyd as conservation consultant. His major contribution was to develop the idea of conservation committees – where FC staff actually met with conservationists to discuss how the forest should be managed. It turned out to be the beginning of a much more open FC, a process that has developed and accelerated over the years.

There was a mixed reaction in the field: foresters did not like the idea of being told what to do by conservationists, but most were ready to give it a try. Conservation committees worked at several levels: basically, and the stated aim, the committees did give advice. Far more important in the long run, both sides realised that the other didn't have three heads and breathe fire. The experience of working with people who were actually countryside professionals rather than the 'real public' softened up foresters for an increasingly wide engagement with people.

There was also an unexpected side effect: far from giving a lot of advice, many early conservation committees ended up with foresters explaining to fascinated conservation colleagues what went into managing a forest. Their appreciative reception of foresters' expertise gave foresters the confidence to let go a little, and become less defensive, so that what had started out in many people's minds as a confrontation gradually evolved into closer and closer collaboration.

Most foresters were in fact fascinated to learn more about their forest's wildlife. Conservation committees faded in the end, for the best possible reason: conservationists just found they hadn't the time to devote to a habitat and management that wasn't a threat – and they had come to trust the people managing the forests. It did create a problem currently rearing its head: it left many of the key players in the forestry and conservation debate, RSPB in particular,

Chapter 3: The New Forestry

without the sort of comprehensive policy position they have on topics like agriculture and planning.

In 1986 I was lucky enough to spend two weeks in Oregon, Washington, and British Columbia with Duncan Campbell and Simon Bell, both FC foresters turned landscape architects. It was a fascinating experience, stunning trees, big landscapes warm and generous hosts both sides of the US/Canadian Border and much to think about.

The US Forest Service was in the middle of its own 'Flow Country' debate – a battle over the conservation of its old growth forests – the spectacular natural conifers of the North West, with the Spotted Owl the Greenshank equivalent. It was a crucial learning experience for me. The Forest Service had lost trust and lost the initiative. I returned to the UK vowing never to get into that situation, even if it meant making far greater concessions to public opinion than many of my colleagues might find acceptable.

The other big lesson, in Oregon, was that where the population was largely urban – this is Boeing and Microsoft's home state – the rural would lose out. Logging employed lots of people but they just weren't going to win against public opinion. In contrast, in British Columbia revenue from logging was too big a part of the public purse and the felling kept rolling on, although it looked to us as if it was not sustainable.

On sustainability, we were faced with a big issue for forestry generally: foresters claimed what they were doing was sustainable simply because trees were being replanted but the contrast between the old and the new was extreme: old growth conifer forest is extraordinary – giants, often Douglas Fir but also Western Red Cedar and Western Hemlock – tower out of sight. Fallen trees create the glades in which deer feed and in the gaps, even on the rotting trunks themselves, new trees shoot towards the scarce light. Everything is covered in mosses and lichens – this is temperate rainforest, bathed not just in rain but in the Pacific mists that sweep in to blanket the landscape.

Replanted old growth is a Douglas Fir plantation, no different from what you can see in the Forest of Dean. Our Douglas is better thinned and sometimes even has remnant ancient woodland flora like Bluebells, adding a dash of colour. American plantations were dark, regular and bore no relationship whatsoever to what they replaced. They were as similar to old growth as a plantation of Norway Spruce is to an ancient East Anglian coppice with standards.

Two further lessons from the US proved very valuable back in Britain. FC had tried a range of site-planning systems for its planting and harvesting operations but none really stuck. Under their legislation, the United States Forest Service were obliged to produce project plans for major works and we saw one for a river project. It solved one of our big problems: how to ensure that each concern within the different aspects of forest management was properly taken into account – harvesting-led plans often ignored the subsequent planting, and road engineering and wildlife were usually ignored. In South and West England Region we introduced the inelegantly named 'Operations Instruction 1' – environmental site planning. It had a section for everyone involved in an operation to complete and was signed off by the District Manager who balanced out the different interests and made the final decision over conflicts. This one stuck and went far further than just the environment: for example, forestry equipment touching high voltage power lines is the cause of some of the most serious accidents in forestry. In the 2000s it became apparent that almost all accidents were occurring where machines were working on unplanned sites like small patches of windthrow: on the sites with full plans accidents had been eliminated because hazards were clearly marked and the site was planned to avoid them. Today technology has taken the battered handful of working papers of the 1990s a leap forward: the plan is on screen in front of the harvester operator, the harvester automatically records the volume and specification of timber it has cut, it is mapped by GPS and available on screen back at the forest office.

Chapter 3: The New Forestry

The other innovation, still in use today, was the use of encapsulated signs explaining what is happening on a works site – equally elegantly named 'temporary operations signs'. An early example of real community engagement, signs included the name and phone number of the forester responsible, not just an anonymous office number, and explained what harvested timber would be used for, which trees had been planted after felling, and why a walk might need to be closed for a few weeks.

What became the foundation of a new approach to forestry had in fact been laid a decade earlier in Kielder Forest in the late 1970s. Under Tony Spencer's leadership, Kielder had been experimenting with a way forward as felling accelerated. Landscape plans had been developed for some prominent views but they didn't seem to tackle the two big issues:

First, that people hated the huge areas of closed, dark, even-aged, spruce which felling at economic age would simply re-create.

Second, felling in age sequence looked certain to repeat the windthrow problems of the first rotation, with trees blowing down in sequence from the west.

The foresters took the decision to take the forest by the scruff of its neck and simply change it: restructuring was born, and a decade later was so embedded that it was enshrined in the 1990 Nature Conservation guidelines.

At the heart of restructuring was a planned breakup of the even-aged blocks by felling some stands before their economic felling age and some after. This lost a significant amount of money because trees rise in value disproportionately in their last few years, as most new volume is valuable sawlogs rather than cheaper pulp. The penalties are less severe when trees are retained, but in Kielder the problem was whether they would blow over as windthrow increases with height.

Bob McIntosh, as District Manager, became the leading proponent of restructuring, promoting it throughout FC and changing Kielder's public image in the process. The forest is a very different place today, halfway through the next rotation with the differing ages of trees clearly visible in the landscape. It is not a process that can be completed in one rotation: at each felling the gap will be stretched until there is what is described as a 'normal' forest, stand ages spread across the rotation so an equal amount of timber matures each year.

To keep retained trees standing Kielder used forest roads and streams as 'hard edges' where trees already on the outside of stands resisted the wind better than trees newly exposed as neighbours were felled. This did limit landscape improvement compared with the less-wind-vulnerable sites I worked on in Yorkshire.

Whilst age class is at the core of restructuring it went a good deal further. More open space and more broadleaved trees were the two leading ways of improving the forest's ecology and the forest's appeal to the visiting public. Watercourses were the obvious open space and they were designed in scale with the landscape, often quarter-mile wide on these huge, gently rolling, hills. They were also a good place to plant broadleaves because soils were better and, of course, it opened up the watercourses – avoiding conifer shading and giving lots of space for runoff.

I was very interested in what happened to birds when the trees were felled: the prevailing wisdom was that planting simply wrecked the habitat and that the special birds of open ground contrasted with common species of the conifer forest. Felled areas seemed to be a wasteland of jumbled branches, clearly no use to wildlife. In fact, many species of the open ground did come back to the felled areas, but not all, and some of them were exciting: in Northumberland the plot I surveyed had both Black Grouse and Short Eared Owl, now much rarer, and a far-higher density of Meadow Pipit than the open hill. In Yorkshire I became interested in the enigmatic nocturnal Nightjar, a few of which were found on felled areas. We discovered 50 pairs (over 200 now) just in time for the 1982 British Trust for Ornithology (BTO) national survey, leading to observers being directed to felled forest, previously seen as

Chapter 3: The New Forestry

no more than a curiosity for Nightjar. This resulted in over half the national population being found on forest clearfells, and Nightjar became symbolic of restructuring and the continuous supply of new open habitat it generated. It was increasingly recognised that the forest cycle – with different stages of forest always there – maintained the highest level of species, with additional features like broadleaves and open streams providing specific habitat for further birds.

In Yorkshire we followed with the first restructuring plans outside Kielder. I worked with Brian Stockdale on Newtondale, the spectacular glacial valley in Cropton Forest, and with Geoff Haw on Dalby. The impact of the restructuring now greets forest-drive visitors to Dalby at the top of Pexton Bank, looking across the dale to the varied age stands on the valley side. Limited windthrow meant we could keep more trees to grow on to stately giants in the Yorkshire forests.

The message of restructuring – that it is possible to make a huge change to tackle big problems – has not only transformed the early forests but has inspired FC's imaginative approach to an increasingly wide range of land-management challenges. It quite simply is possible to break out of the bounds of how things have always been done and take a completely new view. We can restore habitats, move trees from place to place and create new landscapes. Its implications are vital as we face the challenge of climate change, but they are poorly understood amongst the siloed, single-purpose, interests that dominate the debate today.

The scope of forest re-designs and planning has expanded dramatically since the early days of restructuring: a much-wider range of silvicultural approaches, especially continuous cover and natural regeneration, greater recognition of broadleaves and of the value of open space and, of course, habitat restoration. Restructuring started from a position of solving a range of very different problems. It became the basis of FC's ability to plan for many different concerns at the same time.

Forest Vision

Environmentalists pointed out the problems with British forestry – quite accurately on the whole, however uncomfortable for the foresters – but it was foresters who largely solved them. The Environmental sector's prescriptions were generally an either/or: if something is bad, stop doing it. Foresters looked for the third way: novel thinking to generate more benefit, a whole larger than the sum of its parts. That skill, a skill which many commentators don't understand and therefore don't recognise, looks increasingly valuable and vital. The either/or sums don't add up. There just isn't the space in the UK. We have to do better; and 30 years of multi-benefit land management planning expertise could be FC's greatest value to the nation, greater even than the forests themselves. Our wider national land-use thinking today needs to absorb the lesson from 1985 that the whole forest – and the whole landscape – has conservation value.

The big plans for huge forests create a new and varied structure at a landscape scale, but much of the beauty and sense of place is a product of the small-scale internal landscape in which people actually walk. Very small features – the design of a ride, a special feature tree, a hulking old veteran in a neat plantation of younger trees – make the difference: they create the sense of place that makes woodland unique and special. They are the antithesis to the regular wall of planted Sitka Spruce lining mile after mile of forest road. An attractive forest at the walking scale is impossible to plan in an office in the way big landscapes can be designed: it's up to the men on the ground. Managing edges started with conservation projects – ride side management, with bays cut back into the trees, and 'diamonds' of open space at ride intersection for butterflies in forests like Haugh Wood and Bernewood in the 1980s. Conservation management could be rather geometric but it did open up woods and create variety.

Led by Oliver Lucas in Dorset, the men who marked the trees for felling – the people who really shaped the look of the forest – have increasingly been trained and given the leeway to create more

Chapter 3: The New Forestry

interesting edges. The hard constraints minimising the amount of open land that wouldn't produce timber have been lifted. Some stunning edges have resulted: pulling trees back from the ride or path side (but not in regular straight lines) 'pinch' points where the trees come back together concealing the next view, big broadleaves 'drawn' out of the surrounding forest by thinning away smaller trees around them are just some examples. Like so much of forest design the big problem for both designers and foresters is that the best design looks so natural they can be taken completely for granted!

It is a characteristic of state forests around the world to try to make all their land conform to a common standard. In England it was the upland conifer forest exemplified by Kielder. Inspired by the organisation Common Ground, we set out to reverse this with a programme called 'Forest Distinctiveness', aiming to restore the individual character to forests by playing to whatever is particularly special about their landscape, trees and wildlife. It did not last long as a policy drive, perhaps due to the snappiness of its title, but the thinking lasted, with an increasing effort in all our strategic planning to draw out the special character of each forest.

So has restructuring worked? Has it achieved its main aims? In a way it's not for me to judge; I, like most of my FC colleagues, am too close – it's our baby and hard to be objective. Windthrow is the more solid, objective, indicator but there has not been that much wind in the uplands since the late 1980s. The one serious storm in England hit the Lake District, and in Grizedale Forest it is clear that the varied age class of restructuring did limit damage – in one example up on the top of Grizedale a mature compartment blew completely. However, when the wind hit a mature Scots Pine retention (trees kept well beyond theoretical felling age) on a drier knoll and a thicket stage stand just 15 years old the windthrow stopped, exactly as planned.

Restructuring certainly created a more varied and interesting forest: gone were the endless walls of even-aged stands. Some variation could be seen as rather regular – you can see the planning at Kielder. A more varied approach to silviculture – especially mixing in continuous cover – will improve the forests even further. Walking in the forest, even in a simple felling and planting system, is far more attractive, especially where in low windthrow areas boundaries sweep across roads and paths and 'freeform' rounded and sculpted edges are possible. In some ways restructuring hasn't lived up to its promise for birds, with some of the exciting birds of the upland restocks disappearing – Short Eared Owl and Black Grouse in particular – and 'possibles' like Hen Harrier in the uplands and Stone Curlew in East Anglia not making it on to restocks. However, the reason for the absence of at least the Owl and Grouse may well be due to the return of the Goshawk rather than the wrong habitat. Nightjar and Woodlark have become defining species of restructuring in lowland conifer forests, with the Thetford Forest Special Protection Area's management plan based firmly on restructuring's continuous delivery of suitable habitat.

For me personally, the most exciting part of working for the Forestry Commission was the design of large landscapes and ecosystems: FC's huge land holding, its delivery ability and the imagination of its staff, combines into a unique capability. In particular, the challenge of balancing all the demands on a piece of land to extract maximum benefit for wildlife, landscape, timber, heritage, local employment and recreation contrasts sharply with the political norm of opposing forces: either you are commercial, or you are for wildlife, or for people but never all combined. Again, this is the special skill at which FC excels today.

Chapter 4

Recreation

I arrived in Bristol in 1988 charged with environment management in the southwestern third of the country. The FC's reputation had never been lower – despite being two countries away from the scene of the action, the 'Flow Country' still dominated any discussion about forestry. That didn't stop the southwest's forests being as popular as ever with millions of visitors every year. The Forest of Dean had been one of the first areas to develop access and its first-generation provision – buildings, furniture, car parks – were worn down with use. Benches warped almost to the ground, picnic tables worn away, rotting and burnt, leaking Portakabin toilet blocks bought 15 years earlier with a 15-year design life. With the Conservancy's newly appointed landscape architect, James Swabey, who has played a pivotal role in design and recreation planning, I set out to try and bring recreation up to date.

The Forestry Commission has a quite spectacular history on access and recreation, reflecting the sheer vision of which the organisation is capable. The Forestry Commissioners declared the first forest parks, Argyll and the Dean, before the 2nd World War. England and Wales had to wait another decade for their national parks, Scotland far longer. Although forests were initially kept shut because of fire risk, from the 1960s all forests where FC could give legal access were opened to people. Deeply embedded traditional opposition to public access spread well beyond private land, affecting even charities and local authorities. The Forestry Commission I joined was the opposite: you had to argue to keep people out, not let them in.

Forest Vision

Almost invisible, is this perhaps FC's greatest value, its real gift to the nation? That deep-seated philosophy has turned the forests into the place inexperienced countryside visitor feel safe, where they don't have to know how to read a map, and know they aren't going to get thrown off the land. Through management invisible to people who have simply come to relax, FC uses its space to separate out different activities so people can find peace, or excitement, without falling over each other.

Once the forests were open, development to welcome people went ahead rapidly. Signature features included the threshold signs that have become synonymous with open access, loose-surface car parks sculpted amongst the trees, rather than crude urban tarmacked rectangles, and forest walks marked with colour-coded fencing stakes at regular intervals. Information leaflets, toilets and visitor centres followed. Recreation boomed during the high public expenditure '60s and '70s. A key policy, to which FC stuck, was no car access to its management roads, other than a small number of popular forest drives. This was vital in preserving the peace of the forest and safety of walkers.

First-generation facilities were aimed at the average user, biased by foresters' interests, especially towards trees and wildlife, with many leaflet-guided 'nature trails'. They were free at the point of delivery – car parking charges were still generally rare; opportunities to shop and eat were limited and any small visitor centre shops serious and book-heavy. This was the era of popular car ownership and the 'drive in the country'. People really did sit in folding chairs reading their newspapers in the meadows along the Dalby Forest Drive and many people didn't venture far from their cars. FC also discovered the art of directing pressure without 'Keep out' signs, because people tended to follow the routes the foresters laid out.

As we thought about the next generation of recreation, we did something that has proved useful ever since: look at the best facts about what people want. The National Household Survey told us

Chapter 4: Recreation

that, after parking the car, countryside visitors wanted good toilets, refreshments, and the chance to buy a souvenir in that order. The serious museum-style displays at the heart of most 1970s' centres featured somewhere around 15th in people's preferences. Leisure spending was already increasing sharply and that has continued. In recent years the obvious decreases in proportion of income spent on things like food have been joined by more surprising ones, including lower spending on cars and even housing, but leisure keeps driving upwards as disposable income increases.

We also realised that 'worthy doesn't work' – there's a limit to how serious and heavy you can be in putting across messages. As foresters, it is our work, but visitors are in the forest to enjoy themselves so there needs to be fun and interest. It is still born out time and time again by deserted traditional visitor centres, and perhaps most dramatically by the ill-fated Doncaster Earth Centre Millennium Lottery project – the right messages, a very worthy idea, but just not grabbing the visiting public.

I inherited finalised plans to refurbish the Visitor Centre at Wyre, traditionally, and expensively. A destination used mainly by locals, it was particularly unsuccessful because repeat visitors came in, saw it once then simply avoided it on future visits. It was our last extensive, expensive traditional display.

The other inheritance was far more intriguing and set off a very different trend. This was the Dean Sculpture Trail conceived by my immediate predecessor, Martin Orram, and Jeremy Rees, founder of the Arnolfini Centre for Contemporary Arts in Bristol. FC had been very much involved in outdoor sculpture, especially in Grizedale which had become famous with early examples of works by people like Andy Goldsworthy. The Dean was different because, in contrast to traditional sculpture parks, each piece was commissioned for a very specific site within the forest, chosen by the artists. It also exemplified a different approach to recreation: there was nothing average about the trail and the works were chosen by people at the cutting edge of modern art, not a forester doing his best in an unfamiliar area. It was an important lesson – one that Ron Hoblyn and I had applied previously to the Thetford Bird Trail, designed by birders for birders.

The Trail was initially quite elitist – you had to find the sculptures in a large area of forest but it soon got so popular that a waymarked trail was essential and after that some sections, not planned for lots of people, became very muddy and had to be repaired. Over 50,000 people a year have been round a trail expected to appeal to art aficionados only and it is still popular today, with new pieces being added. Its starting point at Beechenhurst, the old colliery pit head, developed as the 'heart of the forest' in the early days of the Dean Forest Park was the second major project we undertook to re-develop recreation in the south west.

The first project was at the world-famous Symonds Yat viewpoint in the Forest of Dean. It was built with public money, already scarce even before timber prices crashed. The plans were all ready and we were ready to go with a re-designed car park and toilet block, when it was pointed out that the whole project was located on a scheduled ancient monument: not a good start and back to the drawing board. A blessing in disguise, we debated whether people would walk the 400 metres from outside the walls of the Iron Age hill fort to the viewpoint. However going there gave much more space and James Swabey designed what's still probably the most attractive car park, and a lavish toilet block complete with a big sink for the muddy rock climbers (and now mountain bikers).

Beechenhurst came next; a much-larger building with toilets, café and shop, and a large car park. Only half joking, I described it as a self-financing toilet block – toilets are very expensive to maintain in a good, clean condition. Staff on site making money was a good start to reducing net cost. Like all the subsequent projects, we struggled for money – the building was built to budget, not need. In every project we looked around for ideas and inspiration. The building was oriented so that, as you walked through the open arch at its centre, you emerged to the view of the huge sculpture

Chapter 4: Recreation

Place – better known as the Giant's Chair – at the top of the hill above. A path wound upwards, luring visitors up the steep slope to the forest, previously a barrier to leaving the picnic site. Built in Dean stone, wood and wood shingles, the original design lacked something until Andy Berzins, architect of the successful Westonbirt Arboretum Centre, curved the straight building and so simply transformed it. A key principle was that the building was a service to the natural environment, not an end in itself like many architect's statement visitor centres. Beechenhurst was particularly successful at disappearing into the landscape: from the building there is a superb, focussed view of the Giant's Chair. But from the Giant's Chair with leaves on the trees in summer you can see neither building or car park at all.

We had a lot of rotting furniture; much of it unsafe as well as unsightly. Some had been put together locally with wood and six-inch nails. Better designs were inspired by Grizedale Chief Forester Bill Grant's introduction of US Forest Service designs following a hugely influential Churchill Scholarship in the 1960s. He brought back lots of ideas, including the ubiquitous 'A-frame' picnic bench but they were looking old 30 years on. James Swabey and Dean Recreation head John Anderson, a keen woodworker, set to and designed new furniture. We tested it ourselves – which was fortunate, as the back of the first seat design was excruciatingly in the wrong place.

The new furniture was chunky, twice the dimensions of normal picnic furniture. There were four reasons for this. FC is about wood – and we wanted to demonstrate its use. Park furniture looks slight and out of scale in a forest setting – these seats fitted their environment as well as making a clear statement that this was a rural forest, not a town park. The weight of wood meant the furniture would be safe for far longer, with minimal risk of rot; and, finally, for a very modest increase in cost, the resistance to damage was increased several times, to the extent of putting off all but the most persistent vandals.

Forest Vision

The furniture was designed to be as simple as possible, with a minimum of joints and fittings. It has become standard now throughout the FC in England. Design has played a key role in upping standards: generally, we wanted furniture to sink into the background rather than be a feature in its own right. It is the forest people come to visit and in too much of the countryside man-made artefacts jar – from rotting woodwork to metal urban signage. This was the base standard, but better design, artist carved seats, for example, are always welcome as are quality regional designs like the split chestnut fencing used in many woods in the south east.

However, one of the most destructive creatures in the countryside is the recreation ranger with a hammer and 6-inch nails. Not only are the proliferating products of this awful predator badly designed, ugly and ubiquitous, but also an accident waiting to happen when all too soon the rail rots off its post and some poor kid gets gashed by the sticking-out nail as they dash around burning off energy.

In 1988 FC had its fair share of quaint, rotting benches, which is why we issued an instruction – and there were not that many direct orders – to simply remove all the old woodwork from the forest before someone got hurt. South East England was particularly bad and it became a management game over several years, with the keen participation of local staff led by David Williamson, a stickler for neatness, to see if I could spot ones they'd missed. Design, and appreciation of what it does for the quality of the visit, became endemic throughout FC in a way that simply doesn't seem to happen in other bodies – the National Trust and RSPB, for example, have some excellently designed signs, gates and furniture but have failed to latch onto a national standard: in particular, the variety of materials varies greatly, swinging from wood to plastic and back again. Even they suffer from the activities of unsupported local staff which can lower quality dramatically.

Some local authority run country parks are particularly bad: in one I counted 12 sign structures without moving my feet, added

Chapter 4: Recreation

one after the other without any apparent thought to the visual pollution they caused. Why do so many country parks decorate the crucial threshold where visitors arrive with giant wheely bins? What this tells me is that these are cosy worlds where the visitor has been pushed to one side for the convenience of the staff, for whom the park really seems to be run. A general campaign to remove at least one rotting structure for every one added would be a great leap forward on most rural recreation sites.

Each piece of design added to a portfolio of quality products that could be used by other new projects: whilst they could always be improved on, it did make it easier to achieve a basic, consistent, standard without having to continually reinvent the wheel – and that left more time for new ideas.

Our first paths were a case in point. The FC's civil engineers had built the largest network of non-public roads in Britain and are the national experts in loose gravel surfaces. For the sculpture trail they specified a miniature version of these 40-tonne timber roads: proper foundations grading up to smaller and smaller sizes, finishing in a fine 'dust', definitely not the pea gravel favoured by many recreational path builders – just try pushing a wheelchair through pea gravel. Properly cambered and constructed paths do not need wood coping down the side – that is a clear sign of poor specification, almost certain to sag and puddle in the middle rather than shed water.

The first path was built with a JCB. A beautiful path, spot on spec – but, unfortunately, sitting in a sea of mud twice its width either side. The next path used a mini-digger, recently introduced in the late 1980s. The whole job was done within the width of the machine, not a mark on the grass either side, and from that a system developed which went on to build over 70km of wheelchair-friendly paths in a year during the Capital Modernisation Fund programme.

The quality of the stone was critical too – we could not understand problems with an early path at Wyre Forest until we realised stone of variable sizes had been separated out by the vibration of the dumper truck, leaving big stones at one end, and small at the other of each dumper run.

Despite what the Household Survey told us, as good 1970s public servants, we were nervous of taking money off forest visitors – we saw it as a 'rip off'. It took time to realise that visitors might be happy to pay for shopping, or for activities such as bike hire. Funding the modernisation of recreation facilities meant raising more money: first, seeking external grant-aid type funding for capital projects, and second revenue funding from forest-based businesses, whether FC or privately run.

Initially, car parking charges were introduced as they became the norm in towns (stories of worried visitors searching for non-existent meters swung our view). But the target was for discretionary spend to be more important because that gave people choice over how they spent their money. Where car parking charges were introduced there are always low-cost season tickets for local people. Agonising over open access, the aim, wherever possible, is to have a simple, free car park not too far from big, charged facilities. This eventually led to a conscious split: reducing the facilities (and therefore maintenance costs) at smaller car parks and boosting what was available at larger, developed sites. What we lost were the 'in between' sites with some facilities that cost a lot to run, but had no prospect of making any money.

As the developed sites are used mainly by visitors from outside the area who positively welcomed the facilities, and smaller sites by locals wanting a peaceful, undeveloped forest, it has generally worked out well. Waymarking of walks was discontinued in smaller local use woods because visitors knew the woods well and had their own favourite walks. For a long time local use, especially 'doorstep woods' close to where people lived, were ignored by FC: the focus was on the day and overnight visitor, the post-war car tourism. However, when studies of local use woods were eventually carried out they showed just how important this local, accessible

Chapter 4: Recreation

countryside can be in people's lives, with some dog walkers visiting literally every single day. It is about much more than the slightly disparaging term 'recreation' suggests – it can be a central part of peoples' lives and personal identity. It goes some way to explain why people felt so passionately about the forest sales proposals.

The Forestry Commission had established a partnership with East Dorset District Council to create a new country park at Moors Valley. East Dorset – the eastern fringes of Bournemouth – was one of the fastest-developing urban areas in Europe in the 1980s. Moors Valley was exactly the sort of undistinguished small wood that might otherwise have been sold. East Dorset built a visitor centre: water-balancing lakes, the original reason for the park, provided an attractive feature and they also built a golf course. With the District Officer, Oliver Lucas, who is a forester and landscape architect and author of the standard textbook on forest landscape, we thought first about an art project but, inspired by work he had done at Grizedale in the Lake District, settled on a play trail by Andy Frost. Andy creates the most extraordinary fantasies for children and adults from wood, scrap and who knows what. The trail was not a playground: it was a loop through the forest and for any parent who has failed to get young children walking it was the complete solution. Castles, the crocodile pool, Charlotte the spider's web, the snake tunnel linked to the heath's smooth snakes: a wonderful fantasy world grew up and in its first year shot Moors Valley into the top ten new rural attractions, with an eye-watering 800,000 visits. Opened by Esther Rantzen in 1990, over 20 years on it is just as popular today.

Watching children on the play trail started a train of thought that became increasingly important over the years to come. Of course it was lots of fun, but it was also impressive to watch children experimenting and gaining physical confidence in a safe environment – the drops weren't big and there was thick bark underneath. We realised that actually height isn't vital to excitement – it is the concept of the drop, as much as the height, that counts, especially when two large wooden crocodiles are swimming through the bark below ready to devour any kid who falls off. The crocodile pool crossing was quite narrow and difficult – how would some of the younger kids cope with walking across? The question was answered on the very first day when a tiny child of about 5 or 6 solved it by not even trying to walk, pulling herself across on her tummy, clinging on tight.

Andy's fantasy world was quite distinct from urban playgrounds, no catalogue furniture, no hard gloss colours: urban playgrounds are great, modern play equipment brilliantly suited to the urban environment; but again and again the crucial idea is to make the countryside somewhere different, without tarmac and street lights.

We also, by mistake, learned about the needs of the parents. The Health and Safety Executive insisted that the site of each play feature must be defined, so chunky round rails were installed and immediately adopted by accompanying parents who were able to sit chatting whilst supervising their children's play. Even when car parking charges were introduced, Moors Valley was a really huge hit with families, quite out of proportion to the £70,000 the play trail had cost to build. Maintenance became vital as even big, thick steel swing shackles wore out under the pressures of hundreds of thousands of children. The greatest accolade was parents discussing Moors Valley in the same breath as Legoland – quite an achievement!

Probably the biggest mistake James Swabey and I made followed Moors Valley: too perfectionist, we felt we had to do something different each time. What we should have done was roll out versions of the play trail as quickly and widely as we could. Later with cycling, Go Ape and activity centres such as Haldon and Bedgebury the lesson was learnt. It is a pity on two levels – so many more families could have had the fun kids in East Dorset had, and it could have had a big impact on FC's finances.

The next big development was cycling. Mountain bikes were still quite new but were growing in popularity. There's a view

Chapter 4: Recreation

common to government of change being something that is incremental, building on what was there before. In contrast, we were consciously looking for the 'Sony Walkman' moment: the completely original idea. Who wouldn't have wanted a mountain bike when they were a kid? Or to listen to music on the move? But it took a leap of imagination, not gradual evolution, to create these completely new ideas that are now so much part of life.

FC mountain biking really started in Wales. The Welsh got the crucial decision spot on, using keen mountain bikers to develop new trails. There are three sorts of rural cycling: mountain biking which follows up and down trails both on and off forest roads, downhill cycling which is mad, you dress up in body armour, hop on a special bike and shoot down a near vertical drop. Finally, there is family cycling, generally on well-surfaced trails with moderate slopes. Mountain biking has proved to be a major economic driver in Snowdonia, bringing in a completely new group of well-off visitors. It has the added advantage of being a year-round activity.

In England, the start was in the Forest of Dean. Impressed by the amazing success of the Camel Trail in Cornwall, we sought advice from Nigel Widget who set up the first bike-hire business in Wadebridge. The Dean has a huge network of disused railways: once, amazingly, it had the highest density of railways in England. Both James Swabey and Dean Recreation Forester, Gerry Gissop, were keen cyclists, and rapidly developed a comprehensive network of easy trails. There was a terrifying mountain bike 'skills' area at the Pedalabikeaway hire centre, a private business bringing jobs and money on the back of the trail development, but off-road mountain biking wasn't the focus in the Dean because of the environment and the concerns of local people. Later projects, most recently the fantastic centre in Dalby Forest, have both family and mountain-biking trails, whilst flat forests like Cannock have been great for families. We learned that children will cycle where they won't walk, and a new forest demographic started to develop: the forests had always been popular with families and older people, but the late teenage/young adults were missing – now with mountain biking, and later Go Ape, they came in droves.

All this got us thinking about what recreation really meant to people. On the FC accounts it was always seen as a rather 'soft' area of the budget: nice and fun but not vital compared with timber or even with nature conservation. But just what part were the forests playing in peoples' lives? To what extent, for example, might the mountain bikers coming out in groups from the cities, with their precious £2,000 bikes, actually define a large part of their lives and identities outside work around their sport?

The whole question of children's lack of activity, and lack of opportunity to explore, has become increasingly important. More and more adults are talking about the difference between their own freer childhoods, most recently in a marvellous book *Edgelands* by Paul Farley and Michael Symmons Roberts about childhood in the no-man's-land of the urban fringe.

The forest experience is that, given the chance, kids will choose real life every time. This summer a forestry colleague told me how his daughter had chosen cycling with her friends at the Bedgebury Activity Centre in Kent for her birthday treat and it was definitely 'a best birthday ever'. I find it quite difficult to grasp the significance of this message: as foresters, we feel we are here mainly to grow trees and even the more communicative ones like me are still overawed by the glitz and confidence of noisy urbanites. Even after the events of 2011 it's hard to appreciate just how important people feel the forests are – and to fully recognise the amazing opportunities to tackle some of the pervasive problems of our times. Surely it's vital that more and more, if not all, children are given the opportunity to re-connect with the wild, to take risks, build a den, and explore the unfamiliarity of the countryside?

Accustomed to seeing things very literally, we struggled initially when people working with excluded youths, and ex-offenders, explained how valuable the forest was to them: after all there are no jobs in forestry anymore, so why train people for it? We had

Chapter 4: Recreation

simply missed the point: it is the very different environment, and being away from the familiarity and distraction of the city, that makes the forest so good – not for specific skills training like forestry, but for restoring broader social skills: getting up in the morning, doing a day's work, interacting with people in a positive way.

With greater understanding, the approach to recreation and activity for children has developed – alongside ready-made facilities like play structures, there has been a swing towards providing the means for children to have their own dreams, as children have done down the ages, turning what's available – a pile of brushwood, a log – into their very own fantasy and adventure. The woods are rich for the imagination – from a piece of wood that looks like an animal to imagining wolves lurking in that dense stand of Sitka Spruce. On the Haldon play trail near Exeter the most popular feature isn't the things people have made, it's where a path so small adults have to crouch, dives winding into a deep, dark thicket of spruce – completely, totally irresistible to kids.

At Chopwell in County Durham local managers ran up against a serious problem: teenagers were constructing raised wooden mountain biking trails, and many were unsafe. So, obviously, send the forest work squad in, remove them and ban them, and if that doesn't work involve the police. District manager Graham Gill took a very different route: he managed to get the teenage track builders together and agreed that they could continue to build, and when they had finished FC would approve the new track, or get them to modify or remove it if it was not safe. The day I was there one structure was covered in red tape (literally!), but elsewhere banked wooden trails that had been passed as safe by FC snaked through the woods. The skill and engineering that had gone into these trails was incredibly impressive. I saw it again on Merseyside where I met a group of teenagers, all excluded from school. They'd built the most incredible motorcycle jumps from scrap from a decaying farm (no doubt awaiting planning permission for a new executive estate) marooned in the middle of urban sprawl. It left me just hoping that their skill and energy can be harnessed – they may have reduced their teachers to despair and left school with no qualifications, but there was a real inventive and practical ability there – as well as a pretty ferocious work ethic – just so long as their school record does not leave them to a lifetime of rotting on the dole.

At the other end of the spectrum, in the early 1990s Forest Enterprise took over the two National Arboreta at Westonbirt and Bedgebury from the Forestry Commission's Research Division. They were no longer seen as fitting the research brief and were very much out on a limb, with the added problem that Bedgebury was right in the eye of the 1987 hurricane and whole swathes of the arboretum had been flattened.

Travelling around the world, I realised that the climatic range for tree growth in the UK is particularly wide, stretching from northern species from the Taiga forest zone, which might struggle through a continental summer, to southern species from countries like Mexico which in the same way benefit from our mild winters. Trees from a wide band through Europe, across North America to Japan can be grown. They include some exceptional trees including the giant North American conifers like Redwood and Douglas Fir and the stunning, delicate Japanese Maples, the famous autumn-colour *Acers*. Westonbirt even boasts trees new to science like the beautiful Dawn Redwood from China, known from fossils but not discovered alive until the 1940s, and the even more recent and dramatic Wollemi Pine, discovered in a hidden gully in an Australian national park.

At the transfer, Westonbirt was costing £1m a year and making £500,000. Already famous for its autumn colours with large numbers of visitors, facilities were, however, limited. The shop/visitor centre actually closed for most of December! FC was making good progress, however: the previous curator, well-known tree expert John White, had done a fantastic job of cataloguing the collection, identifying thousands of trees. His successor, Hugh Angus,

Chapter 4: Recreation

developed a section-based management system that gave a level of management control unusual in botanical collections. We started by cutting jobs (through retirements, not redundancy) and improving efficiency – an expensive new grass mower saved two man years of work and some jobs were contracted – but only if they had no potential to harm the trees: so chipping and stump grinding went out, mowing stayed in house. Chopping the odd tree with the mower in a town park is one thing; slicing it off when, as with some in the collection, it could be one of only half a dozen in the country, or even 100 surviving globally, is a different matter.

Places like Westonbirt had played a role in selecting tree species for British forestry but now we had to fight off attacks (albeit fairly ineffectual) from elsewhere in the organisation, claiming Westonbirt was no longer relevant and was no more than a visitor attraction. Within a decade, climate change and new tree diseases were looming large and suddenly collections of the widest range of species were back in fashion.

In the meantime, Westonbirt's popularity grew and grew as it got more publicity, thanks largely to Tony Russell, including frequent appearances as the backdrop for local weather reports. Income climbed and, following the initial reduction, so did jobs. Today Westonbirt just about breaks even on a turnover of £3 million per annum and the number of jobs has doubled, many of them in private businesses on site, real enterprise in action, costing the government less, supporting rural business and jobs, and giving a huge amount of pleasure to hundreds of thousands of people every year.

Westonbirt is a good example of the developing relationship between local communities and the FC: Westonbirt had a Friends group going back many years, but FC also sold parallel season tickets. With the decision that all season-ticket holders would also be Friends numbers climbed quickly but it was with the construction of the Great Oak Hall, a wonderful new traditional wood-framed building, the sort of thing you see on TV's *Grand Designs*, that things really took off. The Great Oak Hall really involved the Westonbirt

Forest Vision

and Gloucestershire community – big estates donated oaks and skilled carpenters ran courses for volunteers (who paid for the privilege!) to help shape the oak beams, learning green oak woodworking in the process. Constant activities today range from Friends' volunteers helping the propagator grow the next generation of trees for the collection through to concerts attracting audiences of 3,000 and ranging from pop to classical and the ever-popular Jools Holland. We ran a Garden Festival for several years: a wonderful event but expensive and had to drop it as it couldn't cover its costs. In contrast the illuminated trail on winter evenings, where trees are lit by spotlights, has become an annual favourite.

It was also a good example of the serious purpose of the arboretum: the catalogue of all the trees is available to visitors and it is surprising how many use it, looking for particular species they want to see. Some people come to see the mature trees in the arboretum to make selections for their own gardens and, with the opening of a plant centre, there was the chance to buy their choice on site. The illuminated trail started as a bit of fun but very quickly, like with art projects, it became clear it too had a more serious side: a different way of looking at and understanding trees. Looking up into the lit canopy of a big leafless winter broadleaved tree is quite stunning: the hundreds and hundreds of branches radiating out, sharp in the light against the solid black backdrop of the sky. Some activities put information across directly, but everything at Westonbirt from botany courses to weddings is communicating the beauty of trees at some level.

Bedgebury was a different story. Established as an offshoot of Kew in the 1920s, Bedgebury is actually the National Pinetum, a collection of conifers with the largest range of species in the UK. Much less developed, there had been two attempts already to establish a visitor centre. There was also the hurricane to recover from. Very early on we had an amazing stroke of luck: the second valley was arboretum on one side, farmland on the other, like an illuminated book faced by a blank page. It also severely restricted access

Chapter 4: Recreation

to FC land – in fact the 800 hectares of freehold FC land at Bedgebury was the biggest unused recreation opportunity in FC in the south east. The land came on the market: FC was able to buy it and a whole range of opportunities opened up. James Swabey sat down and designed a 30% extension to the size of the collection, a pretty rare opportunity for a landscape architect to stamp his mark so firmly on an internationally important botanical collection.

FC won Heritage Lottery Funding to take the Pinetum forward – the new planting of specimen trees, a visitor centre, a car park, better access and a new lake. For matched funding we decided to try and raise funds through a public appeal. It wasn't a success: a government body is always going to start from behind; on top of that we just didn't have the contacts, staff or community base in the area. Despite generous help from a number of people, including Alan Titchmarsh, whom we simply did not know how best to use, we failed pretty dismally, learnt a lesson and nearly had to pay back the money already spent. The whole project was rescued from a completely different direction, Sports Council funding for what became the Bedgebury activity centre.

Going back to the Dean sculpture trail and the extensive arts projects which followed, I still find it quite hard to get my rational, scientific, forester's head round the whole idea. The traditional informative nature trail leaflet telling you just what you were seeing, naming that fern and describing a historic feature, was the forester's norm. Was it not worrying that visitors did not really know what they were looking at? And, worse, sometimes did not actually like some of the sculpture or thought it had no place in the forest at all? Watching people and the sculptures told a very different story. Some of them kids could climb on. You would see families in deep discussion trying to work out what a piece – which at least now had a name in the trail leaflet – meant, what it was really about.

The artists had done a stunning job drawing out the area's unique history, on the one hand a beautiful natural environment, on the other a cradle of the Industrial Revolution, where the scars healed by the trees are never far off if you look. I also realised that the sculptures provided a bridge between town and country after overhearing a visitor remarking 'It's just a lot of trees' – sacrilege in a place where professional foresters could spend most of a morning discussing the history and future of a single stand. I took strongly to a tiny piece made by David Nash alongside his main commission, *Fire and Water Boats*: several small, crude boats hollowed from a piece of wood and charred in a charcoal kiln. Set in a small boggy patch beside a stream they set out bravely to who knows where? You could rationalise the historic use of Dean wood in shipbuilding, the charcoal tradition of the forest and so on. Or just join them and David on their imaginary journey into the unknown. Long rotted back into the forest, I remember them fondly – thanks, David, for what you added to my experience of the forest. The trail also developed into a fascinating, and sometimes frustrating, community enterprise, with a steering committee including local artists and some very different attitudes from simple, linear foresters.

The earliest projects were funded in the traditional way with direct government money. As timber prices crashed it dried up and from the mid 1990s capital came increasingly from third parties and revenue from selling services – initially 'compulsory' car parking charges, but later more and more voluntary secondary spend. It was always our aim to maximise the money that was made from selling people things they wanted, not forcing money out of them for things that had previously been free. The proportion of costs covered, and the quality and variety of service, went up together. The level of achievement was, however, hidden by the rapid decline in timber values – for every extra pound contributed by recreation we lost at least £5 on reducing timber values. It was extremely irritating when people continued to assert that 'timber subsidises recreation' when in fact, in some districts timber and subsequent replanting probably cost more than recreation. The proportion of income to cost went from 30% to over 50% and the big centres where the money-making potential is greatest now cover their costs.

Chapter 4: Recreation

It is informative to look at what happened elsewhere: the local authority country parks most directly paralleled FC, set up with public money in the 1960s and '70s. In contrast they largely failed to respond to the post-Thatcherite challenge, languishing in a twilight zone of gradual decline. In many cases they started far better equipped to generate income than FC, with far more buildings and a large very local customer base. In an era of localism, the problem of very small units and the fact that country park staff were almost invariably managed by non-recreation professionals (often planning professionals) has been disastrous.

It was not just a UK problem: I saw exactly the same thing in the US with the National Fish & Wildlife Service and local state parks, neither of which had managed to move on into the Reagan era. In the UK the country parks are as a result, a huge, strategically located, underused, resource for re-connecting people with the environment. Fortunately, thanks to the Heritage Lottery, it is not the case for many urban parks. The £500 million the lottery poured into the equally faded Victorian town parks must be one of their most-popular and best-value programmes: the transformations they and the park managers have achieved are thrilling: a spectacular contribution to the quality of life as well as character and liveability of our cities – of incalculable value to millions and millions of people.

Lack of communication was a central weakness of FC: we hid behind printed trail leaflets but simply did not tell people what we were doing. Nationally, FC struggled badly with the media. Its Central Office of Information publicity staff have a very precise remit in government, which is to disseminate information, and it does not extend to promotion and marketing. Senior forestry staff tended to believe it was possible to tell the media what to say and had a considerable ability to say the wrong thing at the wrong moment, which made any foray into the national media very risky.

In South and West England, and later across the whole of England, we set up a local media operation aimed at non-controversial stories, helped by several contracted PR professionals who played a key role in identifying and communicating things that people might be interested in. Foresters just do not understand that in an urban society their day-to-day life is fascinating: tree-felling demonstrations always draw big crowds and people are fascinated by the lives of wildlife rangers. The norm was to wait for what we thought was a big event – usually of little public interest – and put out a press release. When it failed it proved it was all a waste of time, so there was no need to do it again. I introduced quotas, a requirement to put out a set number of press releases; the stories flowed and local papers took them up. If they were well written they were often printed word for word. We knew what caused public concern so, instead of waiting for the complaints, we started telling people about prominent roadside fellings and why favourite walks were shut for harvesting. Several areas put out mixed press releases with everything from local events to where tree felling was going on. In parallel, more and more events were organised and we discovered what worked and what people wanted. In the early 1990s my region, South and West England, was putting out 60% of the press releases of the whole of FC GB.

It was all pretty low key but it established links – strengthened by direct community engagement as time went on – with the people who lived around and used the National Forests.

Chapter 5

Habitat

Forestry Commission conservation started out as specific projects, usually for habitat rather than species, and most often adding water and later broadleaves, to the forest environment. They were seen as largely separate from the timber-producing forest environment. Edge management, ride mowing and shrub management along rides also developed. Elaborate plans for butterflies widened rides, with a grassy, annually mown strip and a shrub strip behind. Where rides crossed larger diamond-shaped glades were developed; but many forest managers conceded little, fighting for every square inch given up from timber production.

The 1985 broadleaves policy marked the first big change: broadleaves were still a timber crop, but the emphasis had shifted with environmental thinking coming into play. The encroachment of birds into the productive forest was similarly influential: Nightjars on clearfells and Goshawk nests to be avoided by the tree fellers in mature conifer stands. Gradually the scale shifted into the main forest as well as along the edges, and a massive programme of habitat restoration got underway.

In contrast to farmland and urban development, natural features were preserved under the planted trees. Often no more than a seed bank, experience is demonstrating how ancient woodland and heathland floras can come back to life when the stifling shade of a dense tree crop is removed.

Ancient woodland is the most important habitat in the English national forests. Just 15,000 hectares of the FC's English woodlands are ancient semi-natural (ancient woods covered in the native trees that would historically have occurred there). 35,000 hectares are 'plantations on ancient woodland sites' (PAWS). These are the woods that existed before the foundation of the FC and were planted with conifers during the economic era.

The ancient woodland story is fascinating: at the time the conifers were planted our understanding of where these surviving woods had come from was vague. George Peterken and Oliver Rackham were responsible for unravelling their story, demonstrating that some woods had recorded histories back into the 11th or 12th century, or even beyond, and that their ecology was very different to more recently planted woods. They contained species, especially plants, that are slow to colonise and very clear indicators of a continuous woodland habitat.

However, it wasn't a stable habitat, the towering vision of old trees 'ancient' woodland suggests. Ancient woodlands are the product of centuries of management by man and the commonest-surviving ancient woodlands are the intensively worked coppices. Producing firewood, fencing hurdles and thatching spars, the hazel pegs used to pin down straw and reed thatch, coppice woods provided the essentials of life in the days before reliable land transport. Often portrayed as marvellous conservationists, our ancestors actually looked after their coppices because they would have gone cold in winter without them. Bigger timber (trees allowed to grow on as 'standards') grew amongst the coppice.

Like the open fields of the time, ownership of the woods was not the simple 'one land – one owner' taken for granted today: different groups of people had different rights: the small poles of the underwood frequently a common right for the local community, the big timber standards owned by the Lord of the Manor. Timber was valuable. Many woods were owned by the king or the church and impeccable historic records show that a gift of timber was a favourite way of showing favour, perhaps as a pension to a faithful retainer. Ownership of the woods, and the necessities they

Chapter 5: Habitat

provided, was a complex social system – very much part of our common heritage.

Coppices worked hard: even into the late 1800s records show the short rotations (usually less than 10 years) and high demand for coppice. The newly harvested wood grows fast from the cut stumps as long as it is protected from grazing. Surviving coppices are surrounded by earth banks, part of the fence that protected them from marauding farm animals and deer. As London expanded south eastern coppices were increasingly industrialised to maximise output, a forerunner of intensive forest management. The impact on the land must have been considerable, winter coppices churned to deep mud by horses' hooves. It would have been a messy, intensive, management, at odds with the slightly fey images many people hold from 18th- and 19th-century portrayals of sylvan glades. Life in the woods was tough: the 24-hour watch on the charcoal kiln, ruined if air got in as the soil cover slumped, and the incredibly high piece-work production expected from the makers of tent pegs, fencing hurdles and chairs.

Coppice as a productive management started to decline in the 18th century as coal replaced charcoal in iron making. The arrival of the railways accelerated the decline: tiles and slates replaced thatch, wire replaced hurdles and coal replaced fuelwood. During the 19th century oak bark for tanning became a major industry, but by 1900 coppice as a mainstay of rural life was on the way out and was virtually dead by the 1930s.

Pasture woodlands are the other main type of ancient woodland. These were commons with trees and much nearer the grand old woods of imagination. In contrast to the coppice, pasture woodland's main value was for grazing. Trees were pollarded rather than coppiced, cut above head height so they could regrow above the reach of cattle and deer. As well as producing wood, animals grazed the leaves from cut branches. Pollarding of holly for winter food for ponies was re-introduced in the New Forest in the 1990s. Pasture woodlands were much more part of the grazing common of the medieval agricultural system, much more the 'waste' than the cared for coppices, and, like many heathlands, were enclosed and improved for farming in the 18th and 19th centuries. Because they were grazed, pasture woodlands don't have the special ground flora, but they do have the massive trees, now bigger and more spectacular than ever after 150 years without pollarding. These ancient trees are hugely important for a very specific community of fungi, beetles, and flies of dead wood. Many became incorporated into parks – most famously Windsor Great Park – and Britain today has Western Europe's richest resource of these spectacular veteran trees.

Ancient woodland has become a contested area during the current forestry sales debate. There are conflicting accusations that the FC is on the one hand doing too little, on the other doing too much too fast. Sometimes the same conservationists make both charges at the same time! There have been growing concerns amongst one group of conservationists, especially those who know most about ancient woodland, at the lack of woodland management by some conservation organisations, and even more at the logic used to justify it. It is important to explain some of these issues so people can judge contesting claims for themselves.

Despite the clarity of Oliver Rackham's story telling, even experienced conservationists struggle with the nature of ancient woodland. The habitat is a construct of nature and human activity working together to produce something that is neither natural nor wholly man made. That is why ancient woods covered in trees that would naturally be native to the site is described as 'ancient semi-natural' woodland. 'Ancient' is the history of the site, in theory at least continuous woodland cover. 'Natural' refers to trees and ground flora that would have been native to the site before man's interference. 'Semi' refers to that interference: it is not interference on the scale of felling Oak trees and replanting pine trees, but man's influence has still been extreme. First, whilst the trees are native to the site, they may well not have been the historically dominant species. Small Leaved Lime, despite being the toughest, most persistent tree, has been replaced by Oak because Oak was favoured as the best building timber, cut after cut over centuries, each time reducing lime, increasing oak. Second, the structure of the wood is, similarly, entirely a human construct: the very frequent cutting, followed by sunny bare ground and, as the trees re-grow, a dense dark thicket. There will be other lesser impacts: the wood banks which may have drier soils than the main wood, the sunken lanes of cart routes and heavily disturbed soils from working the coppice and timber.

For a conservation view that worships 'naturalness' this is hard to get to grips with. The added problem is that much of what we value in our woods – Bluebells, Nightingales, Dormice, woodland Fritillary butterflies – are products of the coppice. Even today it is a case of use it or lose it. Although humans have changed the species and growth stage of the trees, forest management has not eliminated the characteristic ground flora of the ancient woods – the plants that colonise so slowly but that are as persistent as the Lime itself. Management must have dramatically skewed the 'wild wood' our ancestors first started felling: far, far more open ground, far fewer big old trees and hardly any dead wood at all, a key feature of untouched natural woodland. You have to travel to Eastern Poland to see the nearest Europe has to wildwood, and it is very different indeed. What affects ancient woodland more than anything short of total clearance is loss of light, and it does not matter whether its conifer or broadleaf: in far too many conservation woods iconic light lovers like Bluebell are visibly in retreat. This is against a background of 500,000 hectares of woodland in England, mostly broadleaved, much ancient, that has had no tree felling for over 50 years and is getting darker and denser by the year. The conventional conservation focus is on ancient woods planted with conifers, but lack of management is an equal issue, and on a scale 10 times larger than the FC's plantations on ancient woodland sites [PAWS].

Forest Vision

The management that produced our ancient woodlands is very much part of our history, both natural and human. These links to the past – and the beauty and vitality of the woods and their wildlife as we look forward – are gems in our natural world, 'critical natural capital' of a value that can be neither reproduced nor moved (supporters of biodiversity offsetting, please note!). That is why conserving ancient woods is so important. It is a value still not widely recognised, and the Woodland Trust are brilliant champions for ancient woodland, ferociously fighting the gradual nibbling away from development and the planning system which still destroys ancient woodlands now farming and forestry have stopped. Every wood produces new secrets, often a hidden history dating back to the Romans, even the Iron Age, because, despite the propaganda, not all ancient woods have been there absolutely forever. Unravelling that history, taking on the role of a nature/history detective, is part of the fascination – the memory of recent ancestors, perhaps still identifiable on a local family tree, working in the coppice. This is history we can experience directly and personally: making a chair on a green woodworking weekend is a link to generations stretching back hundreds of years.

I attended one of Oliver Rackham's Flatford Mill courses in 1988. Oliver's teaching was inspirational: making the links between his 'home' Suffolk and Essex coppices and the ancient buildings of Lavenham, tracking the change from wood to brick and other building materials, visiting the tiny remnants of small-leaved lime our ancestors had failed to conquer.

The Forestry Commission reacted immediately to the broadleaves policy in 1985: no more broadleaved woods were converted to conifers, and broadleaf planting shot up, with a restructuring target of at least 5% in all FC forests. It took much longer to respond to the ancient woods that had been planted with conifers, or where densely shading beech had replaced species native to the ancient site. Looking after broadleaves was one thing: removing conifers a step too far. On the Lavenham beat on the Suffolk/Essex

Chapter 5: Habitat

border, Oliver Rackham's woods, FC forester Simon Leatherdale soon started tentative removal of conifers on a very small scale but his pioneering work was continually questioned: up until 1999 when the issue was finally resolved, he says only one District Manager, Paula Keen, supported the restoration without question. For a decade, ancient woodland restoration progressed on a project-by-project basis like the Dalavich Oakwoods in Scotland, but with the projects growing in scale all the time.

The biggest lost opportunity was the 1987 hurricane. In a total failure of imagination FC set out to replant exactly what had blown over, so Corsican Pine replaced Corsican Pine, Beech replaced Beech and so on; all rigidly planted in the best FC tradition with the scarifier furrows not missing a beat, even when it left a surviving Oak isolated between rows of pine. Wildlife Officer Fred Currie provided the only real relief: he managed to get Orlestone Forest in Kent left to regenerate naturally, and also clearings for Woodlark to be left in the Suffolk pine forests.

Later, an area in the centre of Orlestone was intensively coppiced every three or four years. Because the trees were so small it cost, rather than made, money; but the results were spectacular, producing some of the highest densities of Nightingale anywhere in England. It showed what might be achieved with more management – something Nightingales need more than ever as their decline continues inexorably.

FC finally got its act together in the late 1990s. Led by GB Chief Executive Bob McIntosh, it set out to plan restoration of the whole PAWS area. Between 1999 and 2002 FC Conservation Manager Jonathan Spencer led a survey of 60,000 hectares of the FC England estate. This firmly established the baseline and set the challenge of restoring 35,000 hectares of PAWS. As befits the scale of the estate, this is amongst the most ambitious habitat-restoration programmes ever in England. Jonathan's survey was unique in two respects.

Firstly, as well as identifying ancient woodland it also made a prediction of what woodland type would follow restoration – not easy when all signs of ground flora have been lost under the gloom of a Western hemlock plantation.

Secondly, because there was consensus that restoration should be gradual, a record of progress marking steps along the way was crucial. Jonathan devised a system of four categories, ranging from the best – semi-natural – to the worst – pure non-native trees, with two stages in between based on different proportions of native trees. As thinning – and restoration – went ahead stands would move up through the categories. Systems like this normally stand on their own, have separate data entry and can never be reconciled with other data sets. This one is based on the FC's central forest database. It is updated by foresters amending the species proportions after thinning – a single entry with no opportunity for errors.

We looked at a lot of ancient woodlands along the way. Woodland faces two problems. Although it is our richest habitat in species terms it is too common for current conservation rarity-based thinking and has, as a result, been neglected by conservationists. It is also complex: many different woodland types, compounded by three dimensional management options. The manager needs to know a lot and the neat, standard prescriptions beloved of both foresters and conservationists don't work well. Skill and knowledge are essential and the more you know the less certain you become. The FC's ancient woodlands stretched from swamp forest, through heavy clays to well-drained brown earths, right the way to sandy heathland soils. Generally, the heavier and wetter the soil the worse conifers had done. At the extreme heathland end, especially looking at woods in the south east, it became clear that there was a very different model of ancientness: this was not the protected coppice of Suffolk, delineated by a high wood bank. Woodland had clearly ebbed and flowed with the pressure of grazing and other human activities.

Visiting the Surrey heaths again in 2010 I learned more: like many heaths, these had been occupied by a marginalized population subsisting off the land, hunting game, building shacks and

Chapter 5: Habitat

making fires from the local wood; an excluded people living on the margins of society and the law. The way of life started to die in the late 19th century and was gone by the 1930s, although the settled population continued to visit the heaths for food and firewood long after the nomadic population had gone. Today the trees have washed right over the heaths, even cutting out the views from the hilltops, views now being restored at Bedgebury and on the Tudeley Estate near Tonbridge. I visited one area of pure, regular, Scots Pine being thinned for the first time. It looked like a regular plantation but in fact was all natural regeneration on what would have been heathland.

Where conifers do better on lighter soils, floristic diversity and the richness of ancient woodland tends to be less – eventually grading into heathland rather than woodland. Whilst philosophically purist about restoration, at a practical level I see no harm in some of the best conifer woods – especially the big Douglas Fir of the Welsh Marches and the south west – running forward as mixed woodland rather than pure native species. There is a beautiful example at the entrance to Wyre Forest on the Herefordshire/Worcestershire border where huge Douglas Fir are naturally regenerating, along with a wide range of native broadleaves. Left to itself, the stand will probably end up 50/50 conifer broadleaves, enough light reaching the ground for ancient woodland flora to thrive but will also produce fine conifer timber.

However, for anything but the driest woods the native broadleaves do not have much trouble fighting back. It was only by extreme effort – hundreds of men backed up by powerful herbicides – that many of these woods were converted to conifer at all. All too often broadleaves burst through to compete with struggling conifers. Letting the broadleaves back has been a revelation: their potential to regenerate has been far stronger than expected. Ancient woodlands are tough: the ground flora may be slow to colonise but it is also resilient, with the buried seed responding to the light even after 50 years under a dark conifer blanket. Woods operate on two

Forest Vision

time scales: the impatient human scale where nothing appears to happen, about three years, and the woodland timescale – come back in 15 years and everything has changed, assuming you remember what it was like before. Oliver Rackham and George Peterken both assumed coniferised ancient woods were lost for ever, and have changed their view completely as conifers have been removed and woods burst back into life. In some of the earliest restored woods only an expert could spot there had ever been conifers. Like the loss of the elms, the memory of the conifer times could well be lost within 20 years.

The results of an early project in Savernake Forest in Wiltshire are dramatic. Huge old Beech, planted as a grand parkland design in the 18th century, were massacred by the second, less-known, hurricane that hit the south west in 1990. Nearly 1,000 giants were felled. Instead of clearing them and selling the timber, trees along roads and rides were made safe by tree surgery. Whole drifts of huge trees in the middle of the forest were left where they lay. It was extraordinary to walk amongst these fallen giants with huge root plates torn from the ground, ten or a dozen trees all forced over in the same direction. Even blown over and resting on their branches they still towered 15- 20ft above our heads. As ever with trees, there was still a feeling of permanence: surely the signs of this catastrophe would be here for decades? 16 years later, visiting with Jonathan Spencer and veteran tree expert Ted Green, I hunted for these monumental trees and found nothing more than a few bramble-covered logs, reduced to almost nothing, so insignificant that without the history they would have passed unnoticed. The attention after the storm brought in English Nature experts who found far more of the rare deadwood insects than were known before the storm. Now, grazing with English White Park cattle has been reintroduced to restore the traditional wood pasture management.

It was the place of the worst excesses of the economic era that produced the real drama. The woods of the Northants District had limped on, expensive and unproductive until the early 1990s when

Chapter 5: Habitat

even the limited promise of the hard-won conifer crops was shattered: the Norway Spruce simply started to die en masse, probably the result of drought followed by water logging. The decision was taken to fell it all. The successor crop recognised the issues to an extent: Oak and a Scots Pine nurse, with the objective of returning eventually to Oak. Planted trees struggled in the soggy soils, water tables raised even further by the removal of the older trees. The competition around them – especially the ferocious grass *Calumagrostis* – thrived requiring a further prodigious application of herbicide. It cost a fortune and simply did not feel right but it fitted the conventional forestry model. That was until the first Forestry Stewardship Council certification inspection.

Simon Pryor, one of the inspectors, pointed out that actually the Norway Spruce were recovering and questioned the whole validity of the replanting. To be honest, it was the opening I had been waiting for. Apart from the expense, it was increasingly clear that dosing the sites with herbicide was not a good start to restoring ancient woodland ground flora: as Keith Kirby of English Nature put it 'I don't mind you planting Poplar at wide spacing, but could you please stop killing what you say you're trying to restore?' – a penetrating and helpful comment. Overnight we changed tack completely: planting was stopped and switched to natural regeneration. It was very uncertain how it would work and from the start it was recognised there would almost certainly be large areas where no trees grew. In fact, it was hard to imagine trees breaking through the ferocious weed growth at all. The objective was simple: to re-establish as far as possible a native tree canopy. Restoration of the ancient woodland was the first objective, timber production a long way behind.

Clearly, the attempt to create Kielder in Northamptonshire had failed but this is a heavily populated and very arable area: the woods are provide some of the best walking in the area and people are as important as biodiversity. The Ancient Woodland Project was born; a community approach that led off in unexpected directions.

The most exciting was a major archaeological survey. In these small, undamaged, areas in a very heavily farmed landscape surprises kept coming – from undiscovered Roman remains to the ruins of medieval hunting lodges. A few years earlier Red Kites had been reintroduced and now they became a focus, with CCTV relays from the nest to the FC centre at Fineshade, at this stage simply an elegant 18th-century barn. In time the project led to funding, and the re-development of the Fineshade forest centre in partnership with RSPB as a major new visitor attraction.

In the meantime the trees were growing: 15 years later there are gaps, but there are also large areas where regrowth is close to miraculous. Soon, they will close canopy as native woodland. Ash and Birch are the leading species with some stunning, vigorous straight Ash which will make fine timber – if *Chalara* Ash disease doesn't get them. Birch has always been seen as a bit of a 'weed' tree; a useful pioneer but with low timber value. Now, with firewood fetching £35 a tonne standing (the buyer has to fell, extract and transport) it is suddenly a valuable tree, especially when it grows for free.

The 2011 privatisation blew up the issue of ancient woodland restoration. Woodland Trust Chief Executive, Sue Holden, criticised FC for not restoring fast enough. Over the past decade the Woodland Trust's Tim Hodges has been saying exactly the opposite, criticising FC for moving too quickly. A key and recurrent problem has been the misunderstanding of scale: FC's commitment to gradual restoration referred to the whole estate. FC always expected to use different techniques on different sites, from gradual thinning in some to a quick return to coppice in others. An extreme is Western Hemlock, casting the darkest shade, which FC normally clearfells because it regenerates so freely that thinning leads to uncontrollable regrowth. The common misunderstanding of the Woodland Trust was to reduce the discussion to a compartment scale. This was partly through the lack of understanding of the differences between managing a forest as a whole and partly through concern over the

Chapter 5: Habitat

impact of felling trees on remnant ground flora and other features of the ancient wood. FC clearly understood that it would use a range of approaches, from gradual thinning to coppicing to large-scale ride management and clearfelling, where each suited best – usually a combination in any one large woodland area.

There is obviously a debate to be had. Although the target of Woodland Trust criticism, David Williamson's restoration in South East England has been bold, my view is the opposite: even what they see as excessive scale may well be marginal for many coppice species, especially the butterflies like the Heath Fritillary. Heath Fritillary are more appropriately known as the 'woodman's follower' because they follow the habitat created by new coppicing so faithfully. They thrive in the most intensively managed coppice woods so it is not surprising that they are doing very badly, amongst the most threatened of England's wildlife.

Rewell Wood in Sussex is a rare intensively worked 'industrial' Sweet Chestnut coppice from the 19th century. FC maintained the disciplined working of the regular coppice 'cants' over the years. Every year a new area is cut. There are no timber standards, in fact nothing but chestnut, in this wood. It is one of the last refuges of Pearl Bordered Fritillary in the south east. It is not surprising – and to their credit – that Butterfly Conservation have been unwavering in their support of more and larger-scale management. With partners including RSPB and FC they have recently scored major successes in the recovery of Heath Fritillary in the huge Blean Forest in North East Kent; but coppice butterflies are the first to suffer from lack of management and are hanging on by a thread across most of England, with the added pressure of deer grazing hoovering up their food plants even when management lets the light in.

There is a tendency to assume that conservation problems come from disagreement between economic land managers and conservationists. However, the story of management for butterflies tells a very different tale. The early ride management ideas looked great on paper, but what no one had realised was how mowing resulted in a rapid natural succession from desirable, nectar-producing, flowers to grasses, worthless to key butterfly species. Similarly, 'scallops' cut into the edge of woods started out well but quickly changed, losing fragile food plants and the butterflies that live on them. Deer have been the other killer: at Bernewood in Oxfordshire they simply ate the shrub layer along the ride edges. Even in a growing coppice they may be playing a part in thinning out the growth, making it unsuitable for thicket-loving Nightingales which are declining and moving from woodland to scrub habitats.

FC restoration really illustrates the difference between a forest and its individual components – something that separates landscape-scale management from managing individual woods or stands of trees: the way valleys have been opened up to give spectacular views through formerly dense, closed, woods. Other stands are gradually thinned to favour broadleaves and some retained with no tree felling as planned non-intervention. It's a holistic management that recognises the needs of species of different stages of forest development from the bare coppice floor through to standing and lying dead wood.

FC has also been accused of being 'too timber oriented'. That is an interesting chicken and egg: FC certainly is timber oriented, not least because making a surplus is the only viable way to restore and manage large areas of ancient woodland. Where timber stops and conservation starts is really, however, a semantic argument. If the meaning of the comment is that management affects the site – rutting, messy-looking dead branches etc – this is no different from what has been going on for centuries. The idea that horses had far less impact on sites than modern machines is a modern myth. The bottom line is literally the bottom line: most FC conservation work is paid for by careful timber management. There has never been money to carry out much work like the coppicing at Orlestone that actually costs: work out the quantities and the point is obvious: 50,000 hectares of ancient woodland will produce 200,000 tonnes of timber a year. A £5 subsidy per tonne will cost £1 million per

Chapter 5: Habitat

annum. Discussing making money from timber with an FC forester, a shocked conservationist said 'but that's what grants are for'! Fine for the 2,500 hectares the Woodland Trust is restoring – a different matter for the 35,000-hectare FC target, and a very clear illustration of the risk to ancient woodland were FC to disappear.

The reasons behind some of the attitudes to woodland management go deep: there is undoubtedly the issue of cost, and linked to that technical expertise. Tree felling carried out or managed by people without real forest management experience can be very costly. Margins in forestry are low, it is very hard work to make money as a chainsaw operator, and forestry contractors are inevitably ready to charge the inexperienced or incompetent above the odds. Linked to that is the 'what will the members think issue?'. It is real and serious: it has taken both the FC and private foresters a huge effort and great expertise in the populous, urban south east, to communicate why trees are felled and to gain public acceptance. There's no doubt that newly harvested sites often look a mess and that may be worse where the work is managed by inexperienced supervisors. The scale of Woodland Trust holdings – many small woods – would test even the most expert forest manager; in fact, managing small woods remains a key challenge for both FC as regulator and the private and charitable sectors.

These very real practicalities have driven rather more dubious justifications: that it is more 'natural' not to manage. The fatal flaw is that, as George Peterken has explained in his book *Natural Woodlands* doing nothing doesn't lead back to the 'Wildwood' before human intervention.

These woods get darker and thicker and lose much of the familiar biodiversity of ancient woodland, directly threatening species like Nightingale and coppice butterflies. That is a fact: the choice not to manage is a value judgement, but it comes with consequences. Whilst the biodiversity consequences are hard science, what concerns me equally is that woods are being disconnected from their cultural heritage: a thousand years of history, broken in

Forest Vision

many cases for less than a century by the decline in woodmanship, is now being lost. It is particularly poignant because the low carbon economy is on the verge of re-discovering that history: that we can supply our needs from this ancient resource. Today's hi-tech, woodchip fed, Binder boiler is the direct successor of the faggot-fuelled village bread oven.

To be quite clear, there should be woods – or parts of woods – left for nature to take its course towards what George Peterken has called a 'Future Natural' state. A wide range of biodiversity benefits: Great Spotted Woodpeckers, some hole nesting birds, a huge flora of fungi and a wide range of invertebrates of rotting wood, but it is a question of both woodland type and of scale: there are places like the spectacular Ancient and Ornamental woods of the New Forest that are obvious for non-intervention, but it is a tragedy to see a woodland coppiced for maybe a thousand years getting darker and darker, its Bluebells fleeing towards the light edges, leaving moss and ivy behind in the darkening gloom.

I'm pleased that there is some evidence that both the Woodland Trust and National Trust are thinking a bit more about management; they have much to offer in recovering the fortunes of favourite woodland species from Nightingale through woodland Fritillary butterflies to Bluebells.

Professional expertise – or lack of it – has, I think, been a big factor in these problems: not surprisingly, people will go to considerable lengths and concoct a wide range of reasons to conceal that they do not know what they are doing. A situation not helped by a government/civil service approach which seems almost to revel in its ignorance, as people with 'wide experience' are appointed to posts requiring a foundation of relevant knowledge and agencies are casually re-organised in ways that look designed to deplete the national knowledge base.

Lowland heath was a very different prospect: at least removing conifers left trees, albeit slower-growing broadleaves. Heathland restoration meant total loss of trees, of productive forest.

Chapter 5: Habitat

Heathland has been the main habitat for re-forestation across Europe, from Holland to Denmark and Germany and the vast sandy expanses of the Landes in South West France, Europe's largest planted forest (not Kielder as so often quoted). Heathland soils are very dry, often with hard iron pans preventing root penetration. Useless for agriculture, some people see them as worthless wastes even today. After agricultural improvement failed, conifer forestry was the only way to reclaim these wild places, an insult to civilised man and the proper order of the countryside. Swarming with rabbits and snakes, the heaths were also home to undesirables, people on the fringes of society.

FC's first restoration led by Rod Stern, District Officer in the South East of England, was at Crooksbury Common, Surrey's last site for Smooth Snake but at 30 hectares it was seen as an old-style conservation project rather than a new forest plan.

Large areas of England's heaths were planted with pine. Equally large areas were built on: Bournemouth is built on heathland as are many towns around the southern fringes of London. What remained became army-training grounds. As heathland fragmented it became one of the most threatened of all English habitats, culminating in planning battles around Canford Heath in the late 1980s and the gradual acceptance that this land was heritage and habitat, not just waste. Dorset was the leading battleground, fragmentation of its heaths the textbook example. There had been a long-running battle between the FC and the Herpetological Conservation Trust (HCT) led by the charismatic Keith Corbett who would dress up in a Sand Lizard suit at the drop of a JCB. FC regionally agreed to some small reserves but local foresters fought every inch of the way to minimise the loss of timber trees.

With a change of management and South West Regional Director Roger Busby's support against a sceptical FC establishment, the first heathland plan was developed for Wareham Forest in Dorset and launched in 1990. Aiming to restore over 200 hectares, it was by far the most ambitious restoration plan so far. It looked carefully at the requirements of key species like Sand Lizard and Dartford Warbler: the bogs and wettest heath had not been heavily planted and where they had the trees were failing. All the dry heath had been planted and broke up the other habitat types. Also, species like Adder needed different types of heath at different times of year.

The plan cleared large areas of trees so poor that they would never yield timber but also better dry sites growing good Corsican Pine. Links between sites in the forest and to SSSI heathland on the margins were developed. HCT's islands were absorbed into a forest-wide plan, and eventually over 400 hectares were fenced for grazing to maintain the heath and reduce invasion by birch and self-sown pine. Further projects, the largest at over 300 hectares in the Breckland forests, followed the same principles of thinking carefully about habitat and species benefits and about the practicality of subsequent management.

Biggest of all, however, was the New Forest, with over 1,000 hectares of restoration: critical in conservation terms because rather than reducing fragmentation, this restoration added to the largest-surviving heathland in Western Europe, making the biggest and best even better.

Apart from their natural antipathy to clearing trees, FC faced two problems over heathland. Firstly, once the trees are removed the heath becomes a pure cost. Because FC is still seen by government as a forestry business this poses big problems because it builds unfunded commitments. This issue is central to the current debate about the finances of a 'new' Forestry Commission. Secondly, heaths are not a climax vegetation: held in check by man, if left unmanaged they scrub up with trees towards their natural state as woodland. The joke in FC was that there were frequently fewer trees in the restored forest than on the undermanaged SSSI heath next door. At least, given the money, FC has the technical capability to remove invading trees. Many nature reserves struggle.

By the time the FC's first national plan for heathland had run its course over 3,000 hectares had been restored, as far as we could

Chapter 5: Habitat

tell (other records and figures are still as fragmented as the heaths they aim to save) this was roughly the same area achieved by all other managers put together. FC may have the most potential heathland of any manager – but it is also the only manager with the capability to restore it. The future of further large-scale heathland restoration revolves more around the FC's future mission and funding than any other factor, and with it the ambitions of RSPB and other heathland advocates.

Heathland is the biggest, but not the only, open habitat. Two other restoration programmes changed the prospects for scarce open habitats in England. It really was a last resort for forestry when Kielder's Border Mires were planted: that the planting was all Lodgepole Pine, the species of last resort on the wettest and most infertile soils, makes the point. Conservation forester Bill Burlton led a major reclamation programme, winning funding from the EU LIFE programme. It also solved a problem at RAF Spadeadams electronic warfare range where the MoD had been conducting a weasly campaign to grab back land under a peculiar lease arrangement as FC felled it. They wanted the land open for operational reasons and District Manager Graham Gill solved their, and FC's, problem with the restoration programme removing trees exactly where they had wanted them gone. Restoration involved felling and removing or chipping the trees, most of which were both small and low quality. Then drains were blocked. Like the Flow Country, these are raised bogs. You walk uphill to get to the top; not what you expect on a wetland. The conditions are waterlogged and infertile. That was why I was staggered at the speed sphagnum moss regrows. Within a couple of years branches dumped in drains are swathed with bright green moss and the bog springs back to life.

At the same time, planners were looking at the upper margins of Kielder: it is the nature of the re-forestation experiment on which FC was founded that trees were sometimes pushed too far. Even when prices were high the small size at which they had to be felled meant they were barely viable as a timber crop. So, as they were felled, a new, less regular upper margin is being created with some trees retained, lots of open space, and planting of broadleaved trees and shrubs. It is a better edge and potential habitat for threatened Black Grouse, with minimal loss of timber. At the opposite extreme, right down in the valley, Kielder is also carefully husbanding the limited areas where trees resist the wind well enough to try continuous cover forestry.

Equally dramatic was the action for limestone pavement in the southern Lake District. Here, the planting of Whitbarrow with Corsican Pine had swamped a huge area of limestone grassland and produced a sharp tree edge visible from the M6 above spectacular Whitbarrow Scar. We removed over 100 hectares of Corsican Pine. Martin Warren of Butterfly Conservation reckoned the restoration could double the population of High Brown Fritillary, England's most threatened butterfly. Although most of Whitbarrow was grassland there are also areas of the extraordinary limestone pavement – bare shiny rock with sharp, deep fissures cut by running water, with rare plants hanging on in crevices. Lower down the hillside native woodland grows on pavement, the same cracks running through the rock, roots reaching into the fissures. I did not even know this type of woodland existed until I saw it. Here, coppice glades provide sheltered, sunny feeding and basking for butterflies. The real impact was the view from the M6: suddenly that sharp edge of trees was gone and the smooth ridge of Whitbarrow leading to the sudden drop to the cliffs of the scar was back.

Just as it took FC a long time to get around to a full-scale ancient woodland programme, English Nature were equally slow in sorting out the large areas of Sites of Special Scientific Interest (SSSI) in poor condition. When they did announce their plan to get 95% of SSSIs into favourable condition in 2003 they were greeted with scepticism. It simply could not be done. FC, the largest single land manager, had 70% of its sites in good condition at the start. However, in a biodiversity policy world of increasing complexity this looked a big, simple, target and I left the launch event determined

Chapter 5: Habitat

to make it work, probably inspired by rather too much free wine! The government put its money where its mouth was and allocated the FC estate £1m per annum to do the work, later adding another £1m for the private sector. Defra formed a Major Landowners Group and this, I think, is where FC again played a crucial role. Brian Harding, the Defra official in charge, really had no way of knowing whether the target could be achieved, and was greeted by a chorus of complaints from the big conservation NGOs. They had difficulty accepting that they too had SSSIs in poor condition and raised endless hurdles to explain away their apparent failure. FC, however, talked from the start about how the barriers could be overcome.

Another public body, the rapidly improving MoD conservation organisation, backed up the FC: MoD is in fact the biggest manager of SSSIs in England because its military training land has been left untouched by the ravages of commercial farming and forestry. After many years of hiding behind their primary objective of training the army, in recent years MoD has become increasingly effective in looking after its wildlife. Its EU Life programme on the superb downlands of Salisbury Plain rivals FC's work in scale and ambition. Like FC, MoD had no pride to fall back on: both saw this as a chance to parade our improvement and put the past behind.

To cut a long story short, English Nature's target flew: it caught on in government and with deliverers. FC applied its exceptional planning and delivery skills to grind down problem after problem. When the grant rules and SSSI target clashed it was the rules that changed – a powerful illustration of the outcome-led approach FC has taken to its delivery. SSSI money 'finished off' the New Forest, picking up the problems the EU Life programmes had failed to crack. It was still a surprise when the FC estate achieved 99% in good or recovering condition: fairly early on sticking points appeared that looked like making even 95% touch and go, but perhaps realising early where they were may have been the secret to FC's success. It would have been nice – as with many other aspects

Forest Vision

of FC's work – if the NGOs involved in the sale debate could have been more generous about FC's achievement. RSPB achieved 93%, the balance being entirely outside their control, but rather than applauding other's achievement they spent most of their effort justifying their own position. What would it have been like had it been the other way round ? Whilst NGOs are there to campaign it actually strengthens their hand to recognise organisations like the FC and MoD when they succeed. It looks churlish and mean spirited when they do not.

By far the biggest issue in the whole SSSI story were the upland sites in poor condition – 70% of the total – largely down to overgrazing and linked over burning. It is a credit to Natural England (English Nature's successor) and its deployment of Higher Level Stewardship (HLS) that they largely cracked this huge problem. It is also a credit to the landowners, foresters and farmers involved: private forestry made almost as much progress as the FC forests. Given money to do the job owners, their agents, and their foresters, worked very hard to deliver. Fortunately, much of what was needed met several aims: no owner could object to being paid to remove ferociously invasive *Rhododendron ponticum*. There's a double benefit now as it's also removed the primary host of the devastating new tree disease *Phytopthera ramorum*.

Deer were a particular problem for foresters. Spreading across ownerships, reducing damage could not be a simple one-to-one relationship between owner and funder. Fortunately, the government's Deer Initiative (DI) had just been revamped. For over a decade it had been hard to show results as the DI gave general advice and support across the board, which made its escalating funding bids hard to support. What was needed was proof that the DI's co-operative approach could actually reduce deer numbers. Starting with Herefordshire's Woolhope Dome effort was focussed on a limited number of high conservation value areas. Led by Jane Rabagliati, Jonathan Spencer, and DI Director Peter Watson, the new approach has actually reduced deer numbers enough for young

Chapter 5: Habitat

trees to grow again. It has proved that the money spent achieved real, measureable, results and has provided a baseline for future deer management programmes.

Since the 1990s FC has taken habitat restoration into a new league, operating on a massive scale, using the scope of its huge estate and its skills in large-scale management to really turn back the tide of habitat and biodiversity loss in our forests and woodlands. There is much more to do: can there be the political continuity a long-term business like forestry and biodiversity needs to carry through restoration to its rightful conclusion? That must be a key part of a forward-looking FC remit, linked to a structure and constitution based on continuity.

Chapter 6

Privatisation 1: 1993-4

What started with selling some land when the Conservatives came to power always had the potential to develop into something bigger. Throughout the Thatcher years we realised FC might not have long to live. Unlike most colleagues I realised it could all be very quick: the Iron Lady could have made FC history by lunchtime. She probably did not much like what FC stood for but then as now forestry and FC were third-order issues. The strong Scottish bias of forestry probably helped.

It was not until the latter days of the Conservative Government, approaching John Major's 'in Government but not in power' phase, that the decision was taken to sell. Clearly inspired by forestry investment salesmen deprived of their living by the 'Flow Country', the FC then must have looked an easy target, still reeling and unpopular in the aftermath.

Mirroring 2010-11, a powerful coalition against the sale sprung up very quickly. Key players were The Ramblers, led by Alan Mattingley, the forestry unions and local forest users, most notably once again the people of the Forest of Dean. Just like now, what bamboozled the politicians was the eclectic spread of opposition – unlike most issues this wasn't a neat Labour vs Conservative issue. The dog walkers of middle England rose as one. It made it very difficult to judge, and the political sensitivity was confirmed when Ministry of Agriculture, Fisheries and Food (MAFF) Secretary of State, Gillian Shepherd, gave the first indication of a crack, whilst campaigning in the Romsey by-election, by saying the New Forest

Chapter 6: Privatisation 1: 1993-4

would not be sold. The Liberal Democrats went on to take the seat off the Conservatives and after that the whole privatisation edifice crumbled.

It is interesting that the issues never became as complicated as in 2011. I do not recall any mention of limits on what could be sold, or suggestion of primary legislation. But the pattern of events – if less spectacular than what happened later – was identical, with the potential for forest sales, which had been progressing smoothly, severely compromised by the public's sensitisation to the whole issue.

Then as now, there were many people who just assumed that because the government had said it, it was inevitably going to happen – which fuelled my scepticism from the start this time round, and demonstrated it was not just the government who had completely lost the lessons as most NGOs accepted, if reluctantly, the government line.

Chapter 7

Land and Timber

Forest Certification was born from the crisis in the Pacific Northwest of the United States. Certification developed to provide assurance to the consumer that the goods they bought were not destroying forests. The first certification body, the Forestry Stewardship Council (FSC), is governed by environmental, social and wood production groups. It is very different from certification schemes where producers get together to make up their own rules.

Certification looked a good route to gaining public recognition that FC was practising sustainable forestry: after the 'Flow Country' an external assessment was crucial to an organisation that had lost public confidence. A friend from university, Dorothy Jackson, was taken on by the Soil Association to look into certification and Roger Busby, who had a broad perspective on global forestry having worked in Fiji, Borneo, Iraq and South America, felt it was something in which FC should become involved. A small group at the Soil Association started going through the original standard developed for the Pacific Northwest.

Roger, District Manager Oliver Lucas and I also showed Alan Knight of B&Q round FC's Dorset forests to see current forest management in action. Alan was a powerful pioneer of consumer environmental assurance, realising early that B&Q customers wanted to know the products they bought were not destroying the environment.

We had just got to the bit where I was explaining that fire as a management tool does not play any part in UK forestry (it does in

Chapter 7: Land and Timber

NW USA) when Roger and I got phone calls telling us to desist immediately. A private-sector delegation had persuaded the Director General of FC that certification was not a good thing for the UK. Certification supporters WWF responded by classing the UK near the bottom of its assessment of global forestry practice, alongside Canada. When David Bills, controversial for his involvement in native forest harvesting in Tasmania but clearly having learnt the lessons, took over as Director General he immediately reversed the decision and adopted certification. An exhaustive and exhausting process to produce a UK standard got underway. I realised just how ambitious it had been to think we could cook one up through our Soil Association meetings! Once the standard was approved the decision was taken that the whole FC estate would go for certification – and it did.

The first certificate was hard work but worth it. It meant examining everything FC did against a demanding standard. For a forest service based on sustainable timber yield it came as a shock for the validity of our timber forecasts to be challenged! Certification sharpened up community engagement in particular. What emerged was that it was happening but without records or system. Beyond the formalities, the need to get plans endorsed by local communities changed the way FC did business for ever and really ushered in the era of confidence between managers and users of the forests. FC did remarkably well at the operational level, largely due to that other child of US systems: the 'Ops 1' site-management planning system. The one dramatic exception was forest management in the East Midlands, described earlier. FC obtained its certificate in 1999, the first country globally (actually, of course, three countries – England, Scotland and Wales) to have the whole of its publicly owned forests fully FSC certified.

Two years later WWF completely reversed its position by awarding its 'Gift to the Earth' award to the Forestry Commission and to Bob McIntosh who, as Chief Executive, had led the whole process with great determination. One of only 70 worldwide at the time, it was the second UK award after B&Q, which had, through Alan Knight, so effectively led the British campaign for certification.

There was a lot of angst about certification, particularly non-compliance which district managers took very seriously – and, like a number of other indicators, became unofficial markers of performance amongst the group. There was a perception that the certification process was rigid, probably because we were used to mindlessly following civil service rules. I found quite the opposite. What became clear in the inspection for the first certificate was the latitude inspectors would give to actions that had clearly been thought through and could be justified: certification, I felt, was frequently more flexible than FC regulation. They also placed great importance on how much thinking had penetrated through the organisation to the extent that staff quickly realised they were being intentionally separated to test whether the official line from the top actually penetrated to the forest floor – not just the foresters but the men doing the real work, including contractors as well as direct employees.

Certification really sealed a deal which had been developing fast between FC and the forest users: it finally formalised the system of plans going to communities before going up the line to the FC regulator. It gradually became apparent that community endorsement actually made it very hard to change plans unless they directly broke the rules. The potential – never a serious issue in England – for differences of opinion between the land management and regulatory foresters to be a stumbling block just about disappeared. The regulatory/policy side of FC dithered about certification through the 2000s, one minute planning to pin everything on it, the next backing off, usually because it was (and it is true) disproportionately costly for smaller owners to access. The double approval was both a nuisance and waste of time and a turn off to private owners burdened with bureaucracy.

From my experience I would strongly endorse Jim Paice's suggestion that certified woods could be removed from FC regulation;

Chapter 7: Land and Timber

but before the next obvious move – saving money by sacking a lot of FC foresters – it is worth saying that whilst the time spent on FC regulation may have been wasted it was a tiny amount of time because certification resolved the big issues before they ever got to the FC regulators.

There's an assumption that if you do more of one thing – recreation, habitat – you must do less of another – timber production. It's rubbish. As I described earlier, timber management at the height of FC's economic phase was not always that good – in particular, thinning was erratic. From the early 1990s, under Roger Busby's leadership, we set out to comprehensively thin the whole estate – simple, but the single most important way of maximising timber value and, actually, making the woods more attractive.

At the same time, we were thinking about silvicultural management of the forest. The FC had unquestionably become far too wedded to conifers, to clearfelling and to planting trees. In the Forest of Dean, the Deputy Surveyor John Everard got us thinking about other ways of doing things in broadleaved woodland, especially French systems based on natural regeneration (trees growing from the seed of older parent trees). Shelterwood, good for light-demanding Oak, involves quite extensive felling. Continuous cover, where trees are grown more intimately and ideally have several ages growing at once in the same bit of wood, can limit the species range to more shade-tolerant species. Both approaches can reduce the impact of harvesting significantly compared to wide open, debris-strewn, clearfells.

Alongside a new approach to regenerating broadleaves, Operations Manager for the South West, Tim Sawyer, re-started their management for timber. I'd been brought up on the idea that hardwoods weren't valuable. The reality was that they take a long time to grow and if you apply a discounted revenue system they are valueless – but if someone else has taken the time and trouble to grow them for you – and we're talking our early Victorian ancestors in the case of Oak in the old Royal Forests – they are worth a great deal. FC was selling into a booming Oak-framing market as traditional wood crafts came back into fashion, luxury garages, grand designs and a re-discovery of the beauty and functionality of green Oak building.

Tim's successor, Brian Mahony, Mike Henderson of St Regis paper, and District Manager David Williamson went on to thin the whole of the extensive hardwood plantations in South East England. For several years over 100,000 tonnes a year were thinned. Fetching very low prices, the carefully planned work at least broke even and had a dramatic effect on the appearance and timber potential of the woods.

But the timber business faced formidable problems, the sole basis of FC's continuing financial problems. Timber is an internationally traded commodity. Unlike agriculture, there is no EU protection from world markets and no routine subsidy. Additionally, in common with primary products worldwide, the real value of timber has been on the slide for decades. Reviewing Forest Enterprise's strategic planning in the mid 1990s Chief Executive Bob McIntosh produced a graph showing the peaks and troughs in timber prices – each peak a little lower than the last, each trough a little deeper.

It was at that point that I fully realised that waiting for a timber price rise to resolve FC's financial problems simply wasn't going to work: other assets, especially income from recreation, had to work. Recreation and land management, with money making opportunities like cellphone transmission masts, produced a growing income of millions of pounds, all swallowed by plummeting timber values.

Over the years there has been a steady stream of outside appointments into the FC to make it more businesslike. All the new arrivals saw raising the value of timber as the key plank to their strategy and all of them failed. The professionals from both public and private sector went on doing what they had always done: watching exchange rates, watching US housing starts and (in the old days) the volume of timber released by the USSR. There are

Chapter 7: Land and Timber

small niches where value can be raised: it is very difficult to compete with US Oak for flooring, for example, but for large and irregular sizes there is a firm, protected market: larger sizes like framing Oak are not imported. However, what has made the real difference is solid, core industry development by sawmilling companies like BSW and James Jones, producing graded, certified quality timber which is taking an increasing share of the high-value construction sector.

FC statisticians produce a national index of timber values. Prices peaked in 1996 at 550 – it had been at just over 1,000 when I joined FC in 1976: 550 equalled £38 million in cash for the newly formed Forest Enterprise England. By the bottom in 2002 that figure had fallen to just £17.5m for the same quantity and quality of timber. The real value of timber had gone down by 5 times from 1976. No amount of frantic cost saving was going to fill that hole and from the late '90s onwards FC was continually in deficit – for five years forecast income went down by about £1m per quarter. No business was going to survive that sort of impact unscathed. The extraordinary thing is that through the late '90s and 2000s FC never had any money at all – most Chief Executives have a reserve, funds to intervene, but in the mid 2000s I didn't even have enough to publish a report without scouring the accounts for some cash!

Declining prices pushed efficiency and mechanisation: in 1990 the FC had just three harvesters, machines capable of felling, delimbing (cutting off the branches) and cutting a tree into lengths. Probably half the forest workers were chainsaw operators. By 2010 FC employed just seven full-time chainsaw timber cutters across the whole of GB, mainly harvesting oversized trees, especially big hardwoods. Mechanisation has meant that forestry employment, in parallel with agriculture, has continued to fall and the idea of forestry for timber as a great rural employer has continued to be frustrated. However, anyone wishing the chainsaw days back should spend a day felling in unthinned Sitka Spruce. Numbers may have gone down but the quality of the jobs has gone up, along with the skills of the operators. Getting the best out of a harvester requires first-class mechanical skills and, from the lofty viewpoint of the cab, the best operators are both well-paid and expert silviculturalists, understanding and managing sensitive stands with great skill.

However, every time foresters saved 10% on costs the value of timber went down 20%. Despite FC grants, far from new woods being recruited into production more and more fell out, including large estates like the National Trust which greatly reduced its woodland activities in the early 1990s.

It is worth touching on the whole issue of objectives and 'commercial timber production'. The term is used by timber-producing foresters to prove their credentials as a serious, money-making business and by others, especially conservationists, as a derogatory term reflecting the worst side of forestry. It currently causes very real problems. Most of the people claiming they are 'commercial foresters' actually, on closer study, are practising excellent multi-purpose forestry with a bias towards timber, but delivering a wide range of benefits. On the other hand, some conservation-oriented bodies have become confused between timber removals for profit and felling trees for other objectives – in particular, to achieve conservation or heritage aims. The movement claiming that to do nothing creates 'natural' woodland causes further confusion. It is a complex situation, not helped by foresters assuming that wherever trees are removed the motives and standards must be conventional timber production. Behind the philosophy, the exponents of natural woods may well be worried about the reaction to felling from the memberships they depend on, or losing money because of the low value of timber, or both.

The price crisis had further, and much contested, implications: the private sector simply stopped felling timber. In 1988 private sector conifer felling in England actually topped FC output at over 1 million tonnes. In 2001 it bottomed out at just over 300,000 tonnes. FC output had actually gone up – during the early 2000s FC was

Chapter 7: Land and Timber

running at just over 100% of its 'allowable cut' – the volume that can be felled each year for the forest to sustain its timber output. Some private-sector timber growers accused FC of lowering prices.

The processing industry's reaction was the opposite – the evidence being the UK Forest Products Association's violent opposition to the government's sale proposals. Whatever the rights and wrongs, without the FC cut the processing sector would not have been there by the time prices recovered and the private sector started cutting again. Alongside the objectors there are also private-sector growers who recognise this. Now, private-sector conifer felling has recovered to about 500,000 tonnes per annum which is probably just half its potential, and as the trees keep growing so there will be a considerable 'stood over' volume accumulated in the forest.

However, timber now faces an exceptionally volatile future due to two opposing factors. The first, in equal parts positive and risky, is the low carbon economy. Wood for energy is already pushing up small hardwood prices, for firewood, and will affect the whole market as time goes on. There are risks, particularly to established wood using industries but, having always been sceptical about prices going up, I can now see a real driver for higher timber values and more woods coming into management. One thing is worth repeating: wood that simply moves from an existing industry to be used for energy saves not one gramme of carbon. It is harvesting wood from unmanaged woods that makes the savings.

The opposing factor is disease. It has suddenly become a major factor for England's trees: Corsican Pine, mainstay of the most cohesive market after upland Sitka in Britain, has been stopped in its tracks by Red band Needle Blight (*Dothistroma*). An endemic disease, it has suddenly increased to infect most Corsican and some other pines, possibly due to warmer summers. It literally stops pine in their tracks: they lose all but the current year's needles, rarely die but simply stop putting on timber increment. There is now evidence that timber quality may decline even though the tree is still alive.

Phytopthera ramorum attacking Larch, Rhododendron, and where there are sufficient spores, other trees like Douglas Fir, is far fiercer, killing trees virtually instantly. Again possibly triggered by climate, it has leapt across the landscape, despite emergency 'sanitation' fellings of infected stands.

However, supporting the climatic hypothesis, 2011 which foresters had been looking forward to with horror turned out very different: the exceptional drought through April and into May checked the spread of the diseases, a very welcome relief, sadly not repeated in 2012, and exploding into Larch in southern Scotland in 2013. And there are others: two attacking Oak, *Phytopthera* on Alder has been around for a decade and, although not of forestry significance, Horse Chestnut are also suffering seriously. However, it is the recent and dramatic arrival, *Chalara* Ash dieback which has the most frightening potential of all: it has wiped out Ash in nearby countries like Denmark and, after Oak, Ash is our commonest native tree. In contrast to the diseases of conifers, Ash are all about us rather than in larger forests in more rural areas.

Future timber production will depend heavily on price: bluntly, prices during the 2000s fell below the level where it made sense to fell. What could we achieve in England? The FC produces about 1.1 million tonnes per annum, mainly conifer, and the private sector 500,000 tonnes of conifer. The private sector could probably produce 1 million tonnes of conifer and if just half the 500,000 hectares of neglected woods, mostly broadleaved, were brought into management they could produce 1 million tonnes per annum. Conversion of conifer to broadleaves and heathland will reduce timber output, and that is reflected in a declining FC forecast, for England perhaps 100-200,000 tonnes per annum across public and private sectors. The bottom line is that timber production in England could probably double without planting a single new tree. At a stroke it would destroy FC's dominance of the timber market, from 60% today to only 30% if all our woods and timber were in management.

Chapter 7: Land and Timber

A key challenge for the future, whatever the ownership of the FC estate, is to see whether we can continue to do several things at once the way FC does today. On a fascinating visit to the Netherlands, my one concern with the Dutch Forest & Wildlife service model is that as conservation went up the agenda timber seems to have slid more than it needed to. There is a risk of that happening in England with any public-sector solution, and especially a charity-based one where lack of technical capacity may match quite nicely the concept that 'we're not commercial foresters'. Everyone would lose – the beauty of the woods, the wildlife and the timber industry.

After the Conservatives came to power in 1979 they quickly started selling FC woods. No one in FC liked it and, at heart, I still don't. However, apart from a few larger woods at the very beginning of the programme, woodland sales have done much less harm than might have been anticipated. The simple reason is that, in its rush to buy woods, the FC acquired many that it was not well suited to manage nor were ever likely to yield much public benefit. As long as FC were left to make the selection of what was sold, sales went remarkably quietly; the lack of public protest was an indication of the limited use and benefit of the woods being sold.

As Regional Director in the mid 1990s, 15 years into the programme I signed off over 50 woods less than 20 hectares in areas like The Chilterns. I didn't know the names of any of them and had never visited them. It's hard to know what has happened to most of these woods – no one has ever been to check. Some stories are known – for example, ex FC researcher Julian Evans bought the sort of classic small wood in Hampshire that FC would just never have got around to managing properly and has put his own stamp on it – not least using it for research connected with his professorship at Imperial College.

It all went wrong the minute managers were pushed too hard – the public were sensitised and reacted to things that would otherwise just go through. The clearest example was the privatisation policy of 1993-4 which had the perverse effect of actually reducing the amount of woodland sold. During the Labour years it went wrong just once, when a demand for end of year money led to a rushed parcel offered for sale in November, and immediate reaction from the public and NGOs as one wood was an SSSI with a dubious record connected with shooting. Out of 6 woods offered for sale just 1 wood sold. I doubt if the sale of Rigg Wood in the Lakes would ever have hit the headlines had it not been for the proposal to sell everything.

There is little doubt sales are off the agenda for quite some time. Which MP is going to volunteer to go first with a sale in his constituency during this parliament? Which buyer is going to risk being the next Terry Wogan, his private affairs splashed over the front pages?

However, there are still woods out there that are not doing much for public benefit. Demand for woods is high, including from many well-intentioned 'good lifers' wanting their own bit of countryside. Values of smaller and more attractive woods have risen very sharply – in 2010 an exceptional 200-hectare wood in The Marches sold for £10,000/hectare, equivalent to agricultural values and a whopping £2 million. In 2013 the average price for good amenity woods in England soared to £14,000 per hectare.

Reflecting this, in the mid '90s Home Counties' woods were worth 5-10 times woods from Somerset westwards, where some simply failed to sell. The wave of value has spread right across the country, with high prices right down into the South West. I do not think FC always maximised values in the past – in the early days at least, woodland traders did very well buying a sound but neglected FC wood and 'tidying' it – spending a bit of money on the entrance and along the rides – and frequently doubling their money within a year. It would be interesting to see just how much value could be generated by being really careful about how woods were sold.

Ironically, as it removes cash value, in small woods a really good thinning can dramatically increase sale value. It might have

Chapter 7: Land and Timber

been interesting to see just how much value a really carefully managed sales programme, with politicians and FC co-operating rather than antagonistic, might have generated – the 15%/40,000 ha initially proposed by the government in 2010 was always too high, especially over 5 years – but might it have been possible to generate £100m from half as much, a level of sales which could have flown? It's all history now – my guess is it will be a long time before anything more is sold and the big forests are off the market for a generation, and should be for ever.

The classification of woods in the consultation on the proposal to sell everything in 2011 was interesting in several ways. It was one of the few elements that had clearly involved the FC. I have been over and over the estate with different classification approaches, most recently working on the economic study commissioned by the FC with the economic consultancy EFTEC. The classes, and the way they were divided, generally looked sensible. Many of the 'small commercial' woods would have emerged as community woods; clearly the amount in this category had been pushed up politically to make more available for unconstrained sale. It was very interesting that only Kielder came in as 'large commercial': even at the start of the process Thetford was being discussed in that category – it still had not registered that the whole forest is a European-designated Special Protection Area (SPA) for birds. The Dalby complex was the other obvious candidate, no longer included because of its massive recreational development. I have to admit these outcomes were entirely intentional: we set out to increase the public benefit of the estate, and moving land from predominantly timber to much wider public benefit was a clear objective – and this classification confirms the outcome.

Also of interest were the number of green (multi-purpose) woods that were there, and not red (commercial), because of positive action FC had taken. For example, I almost put Neroche Forest, in the Somerset Blackdown Hills, on the disposals list prior to the cutting edge HLF funded landscape project. There were several others – Cardinham in Cornwall for example. Suffolk was particularly interesting – Dunwich, again the subject of a habitat-restoration programme with the RSPB is green, but Rendlesham, which in reality probably has greater potential for heathland birds, remains red. It very clearly makes the point that woods that look unimportant now may have the potential for great public benefit once FC management gets to them. At a different level, the Dalby area is an example of changing priorities: when the main recreation was walking Dalby alone was quite big enough. But with mountain biking dramatically extending the range of a day out, the whole forest complex, three or four times the area, extending right up through Langdale to the moors, is the right scale – and that, along with other unforeseen developments in the future, shows how opportunity can be lost through a snapshot at just one point in time.

Finally, there was a sting in the tale of the land sales programme: as John Major's Government approached certain defeat in the 1997 General Election, a sales target of £20 million, more than twice as much as had ever been achieved, was slipped in to the Government accounts for the next financial year. Committed to existing public spending plans, it was a real headache for the incoming Labour Government – until Head Land Agent Mark Thornycroft pulled off a spectacular coup: The owner of a leasehold wood near the M3 applied for planning permission, offering the FC the value of the standing timber to quit. Mark negotiated the trivial compensation offer up to a one-third share – nothing could happen without FC agreement – and just after the election netted £23 million, filling the hole in the budget with just one deal.

Chapter 8

The New Forest

The New Forest is one of England's exceptional landscapes, a place of almost overwhelming historical and wildlife value. Its survival, when other Royal hunting forests are little more than names on maps, is close to miraculous, especially through the last 150 years as urban pressures have built. Today it sits between two intensely developed areas, the Southampton and Bournemouth conurbations, both of which have grown dramatically over the last 50 years.

In a very British paradox it is neither new nor a 'forest' in the sense of a tree-covered landscape like the Forest of Dean. The New Forest was new just over 900 years ago when William the 1st – the Conqueror – made it his new Royal Hunting Forest. Today just one-third of the forest's 30,000 hectares is timber-producing woodland: the largest area, 14,000 hectares, is heathland and 4,000 hectares is pasture woodland called the 'Ancient and Ornamental' woodland. Together these are the 'Open Forest'. Both heathland and pasture woodland are the largest-surviving areas of their habitat type in northwest Europe, landscapes common in medieval times. The timber 'enclosures' form the balance of the area and comprise the land the Crown, represented today by the FC, is permitted to fence against stock to grow trees for timber.

Two characteristics set the New Forest even further apart. The first, of huge cultural and practical importance, is that the New Forest still has a fully functioning commoning culture. Animals let out on the forest by the holders of traditional common rights continue a near-extinct tradition, as well as shaping the ecology of the forest by their grazing. Linked closely to this, and in contrast to almost all terrestrial lowland nature reserves in England, the New Forest is big enough to behave as a functioning semi-natural ecosystem: as the near-feral herds of ponies and cattle graze the forest, scrub and then woodland advance in one place whilst ancient woodlands decay in another, opening up new glades.

The secret of the forest, and what makes it fiendishly challenging to manage, is that its ownership pattern is completely different to the simple 'one property – one owner' that is taken for granted in modern Britain. Before enclosure in the 18th century complex ownership arrangements shared the products of the land through legal rights encompassing all classes of people. In medieval times most people were involved in providing food, warmth and shelter through their personal activity as farmers or foresters, and real wealth was very closely linked to agricultural productivity. In the New Forest that complex web of rights and ownerships persists. The freehold of the forest has been the Crown's since 1086, and is now vested in Her Majesty's ministers. The Crown's principal interest was in the deer – the venison – which provided entertainment through hunting to the king and his court and also the meat that fed them. Linked to the venison is the 'Vert' – the habitat on which the deer subsist and there were complex rules to protect it. The king had a subsidiary interest in the big timber of the forest.

However, contrary to popular mythology, ordinary people were not excluded from the land. They had carefully regulated but extensive common rights to graze animals, to wood and to other heathland products like such as peat and gorse, and the foliage from trees pollarded to provide animal feed. Most of these rights persist in one form or another to this day. Common rights are attached to properties. The property rights for most English commons specify how many animals can be put out but, controversially, not in the New Forest.

In practice a small number of commoners make a significant living by putting cattle on the forest, whilst many more keep small

Chapter 8: The New Forest

numbers of New Forest ponies for personal interest and as part of the Forest way of life. There are a few donkeys and also, in the autumn, pigs. Pannage was one of the great medieval uses of the pasture woodlands: young pigs put out to fatten fast on the autumn acorn crop then, as winter came, slaughtered, salted and cured. They had a subsidiary purpose in hoovering up the acorns because ponies can be poisoned by eating too many. It's an illustration of just how alive these ancient traditions are that in 2013 the system failed with a number of ponies dying of from a surfeit of acorns. How long pigs could be put out depended on the size of each year's acorn crop. To this very day it is the duty of the Deputy Surveyor, the traditional title of the Crown's manager, to declare the dates of the pannage season.

The Crown's deer, too, are still there in large numbers and easy to see. Commonest by far are the species the kings themselves hunted, Fallow Deer. There is a good herd of Red Deer, a carefully contained herd of the introduced Asian Sika deer, and Roe Deer are moving in. They have a significant impact, particularly in the timber enclosures where commoner's stock is fenced out. The FC now culls the deer to an agreed plan to balance grazing pressure.

Most of the forest is expansive open habitat, dominated by heather and gorse heathland. Thanks to the grazing animals supported by a massive FC programme of annual burning, and the cutting and removal of invading pine, the heath is shorter and has fewer trees than most English heaths. Within the heathland are most of England's surviving valley mires (wet ground spreading up the valleys). Along the streams are 'lawns', grassy areas, richer grazing, many annually flooded by the overflowing streams which fertilise them with silt washed downstream. There are also curiosities such as Mediterranean temporary ponds – natural ponds which dry out in summer and hold a special fairy shrimp *Chirocephalus diaphanus*, one of the many British species found only in the New Forest. Encroaching and retreating scrubby margins as well as the very varied conditions created by animal grazing, make this a more natural

Forest Vision

scene than the typical heathland nature reserve, and create the natural edges – between heath and scrub, between wet and dry, grass and heather – so rare in the rest of lowland England. The last refuge of Dartford Warbler in the lethal winter of 1963, the heaths are an exceptional refuge for heathland wildlife, although the iconic Sand Lizard was extinct and is being reintroduced. As farmland waders have crashed to near extinction in lowland England the mires have become an increasingly important habitat.

The Ancient and Ornamental (A&O) woodland is how most people picture ancient woodland: huge old trees, many multi-stemmed from historical pollarding. Dead wood lies strewn on the ground which, because these woods are heavily grazed, is mown flat, and there is a distinct browse line, too, meaning you can see through the forest. The big trees are widely spaced with many glades. With the heavy grazing it is very hard for young trees to establish themselves – look at the holly clumps which often protect a young tree on the way up. The A&O is a spectacular resource for deadwood species.

The timber enclosures are the areas the Crown is allowed to fence and are conventional timber-growing forests with large areas of 19th–century Oak, with Scots Pine, Douglas Fir and Corsican Pine the principle conifers. Whilst there are regular plantations many areas, because they've been managed much longer than most recently planted FC forests, are more varied and interesting with many mixed stands of broadleaves and conifers. At the popular Bolderwood picnic site in the heart of the Forest huge old conifers, kept way beyond the size a sawmill could cut, demonstrate just how big Douglas Fir in particular can grow – and they have two further generations growing up around them.

Most of the Forest is designated as an SSSI, is a European Special Area of Conservation (SAC) and the mires are internationally designated wetlands under the Ramsar Treaty.

The Forestry Commission inherited the New Forest from the Office of Crown Woodlands, which also managed the Forest of

Chapter 8: The New Forest

Dean and a number of smaller forests. FC is the executive manager on behalf of the Crown but it has to work with a number of other interests who are frequently in conflict with both it and each other. Critically important is the Court of Verderers charged with protection of the 'Vert and the Venison'. With significant powers over not just commoning and grazing but also 'planning' issues, the creative tension between FC and the Verderers has played a key role in the conservation of the Forest over the last 50 years. It is easy to see the Verderers as blockers to progress, especially when trying to manage the Forest on a day-to-day basis.

Taken case by case the Verderer's decisions would often look petty and unreasonable to an outsider: how could they object so strongly to the County Council shaving 30 square metres off the open forest to improve a road junction? Unlike a National Park Authority the Verderers are not required to be 'reasonable' in a Town and Country planning sense. But if you add up all the apparently petty refusals over a decade, you find that a 'reasonable' attitude would have resulted in really very significant loss to this uniquely pressured area of public land.

Particularly interesting in the context of the current forest-ownership debate is that the New Forest has its own legislation defining duties on the Forest, especially the Crown's, and providing extra protection – in particular, restricting the sometimes draconian rights of statutory undertakers such as gas, electricity and water utilities.

Today, rights and privileges extend to a much-wider audience, in particular the non-commoners living in the forest and the millions of visitors who come to walk, camp, cycle and enjoy the forest environment. The New Forest is a very desirable place to live with high property prices, and also a playground for the huge urban catchment extending at least to London. Its equestrian tradition – the commoners still round up their animals on horseback – is particularly strong, with many people moving to the area to ride out on the sandy paths across the heaths.

Forest Vision

This is the ultimate community forest and has been crucial in shaping the FC's capability to work with people. When a mischievous article by elected Verderer, New Forest author and local newspaper columnist Anthony Passmore, suggested the Countryside and Rights of Way Act might enable the FC to restrict access for dogs, 2000 people turned out for a public meeting! New Forest Dog was founded – and joined a host of organisations from the Commoners Defence Association to the Hampshire Wildlife Trust in adding their voice to the frequently combative arena of New Forest politics. Outsiders can be shocked by the intensity and language in the *Lymington Times*, the wonderfully antiquated but pivotal local newspaper. At times the Forest makes Westminster look rather cosy and this is a place where public servants, whether it's the Deputy Surveyor or the local MPs, are subject to instant scrutiny and unrestrained comment – when FC gets it wrong it gets to know about it!

Some of the antipathy is deserved: alongside the private landowners who drove enclosure in the 18th century, the Crown had a long record of trying to extinguish common rights and enclose the remaining Royal forests for timber. In the New Forest one of the biggest crises came with the 1851 Deer Removal Act, which was a blatant attempt to land grab from the common rights' holders. Elsewhere there were share-outs between the Crown and the big landowners, with people such as the farm-worker poet John Clare losing out. In the New Forest, however, it was common rights' holders who opposed the Crown but, contrary to popular mythology, they were in fact common-rights-holding gentry and landowners, not the ordinary people making a living from the Forest.

Almost exactly 100 years later the next big clash resulted from FC trying to apply 'economic forestry' to the New Forest. The A&O had baffled modern foresters: they saw it as a wasted forestry opportunity so it wasn't surprising that the FC started felling to 'improve' the A&O and in particular ensure their regeneration as more conventional forestry woodlands. Local protest on the scale of recent events brought the Secretary of State for Agriculture down to

Chapter 8: The New Forest

the Forest to adjudicate. This resulted, in 1971, in the first Minister's mandate: in effect a special remit for the FC in the New Forest. He stopped the felling, the Deputy Surveyor moved on to better things and was replaced by the great Don Small who, during a long reign, changed the forest forever and for the better. In particular, it was Don with the Verderers and other forest interests who agreed to stop cars accessing the forest – amazingly, up to 1970 anyone could simply drive out onto the heaths! They also agreed to limit with cattle grids the range of forest animals which, up till then, could wander up the public road as far as Salisbury. The FC built its most extensive recreation network anywhere, with dozens of car parks and campsites to absorb the ever-increasing visitors as mass car ownership began to bite.

Nature Conservation played an increasingly important role, led by the redoubtable Colin Tubbs of the Nature Conservancy Council, and was the source of a continuing series of clashes with FC, and the Commoners as the principle land users. FC, as the managers, tended to be caught in the middle as both referee and 'Aunt Sally'.

My first involvement in the Forest in 1986 came just after the resolution of one of the biggest battles which was over controlled burning. Spring burning produces a flush of tender young growth, and the Commoners were always pushing for more. NCC were concerned by the loss of the older gorse crucial to the still critically endangered Dartford Warbler, and also the uniformity created by the large burns current at the time. Keeping NCC and FC on their toes was the certainty that, if the area burnt legally fell too low, someone would rectify it with a box of matches at night, something neither FC nor NCC wanted. The resolution was a negotiated burning programme, the commoners bidding up, NCC down, and much-smaller burns – no more than 20 hectares at a time. Controlled burning takes real skill as a succession of out-of-control fires on nature reserves and heather moors has demonstrated over the years. Yet in the New Forest the FC's burning teams go out and burn maybe 400 hectares, 30 odd patches, year after year without losing a fire, and with the confidence of all around that they will get it right time after time. It is a level of skill and expertise which we take for granted at a real risk to the environment – the sort of critical practical issue ignored or brushed aside in the recent debate, not just by government but by conservation NGOs. At the same time, FC was carrying out a massive, systematic programme to reduce Scots Pine invasion onto the heaths and to remove as many seed trees as possible. A 20-year programme of improvement was underway.

FC struggled with the New Forest and for a long time there was perpetual tension between the Forest and the rest of FC, both at the regional and national level. A succession of 'improvers' visited the Forest to try and beat it into line and make it more like Kielder. They quickly ran into obstacles, usually quite hard ones like the New Forest Acts or Ministerial instructions. I am sure my first visit, at the invitation of Deputy Surveyor David Perry when I worked in GB headquarters in Edinburgh, was to gain a friend at the centre. I came, listened and learnt and was still learning 20 years later. Throughout those 20 years I have been a passionate supporter of the Forest's uniqueness and, I hope, have helped to bring about a near revolution in both the ecological condition of the Forest and the FC's relations with its diverse and vociferous community. When Arthur Barlow moved from the Operations Manager job in Bristol to take over the Deputy Surveyorship from David it really marked the turning point: at regional and later national level we had all worked closely together, and active and vigorous support of the New Forest's unique value and heritage have marked FC management since.

The A&O, however, remained a problem for the foresters. Even after they had accepted it could not be turned into productive timber plantations, they worried that some action must be taken to regenerate it: it seemed to be falling apart and dying. Some small fenced plots were planted and much argued over – the issue persisted. The big break, with much bigger implications later, was

Chapter 8: The New Forest

Jonathan Spencer's move from English Nature to become ecologist in the New Forest. A woodland expert, he had worked with Dr George Peterken, one of the pioneers of ancient woodland science, and Dr Keith Kirby, who became the EN and then NE lead on woodland ecology, on the original Ancient Woodland inventory and was well known to FC staff because he was always sent to solve the most difficult problems with private owners.

Jonathan's first task, sponsored by the 'Esso Trees of Time and Place' project, was a new study of the A&O. The key outcome was to confirm that George Peterken's meticulous research did show that the A&O was not in terminal decline: whilst some woods were struggling others were recruiting new trees well, and overall what was happening reflected functioning natural processes. It was also clear that there were periods where trees reduced and gaps opened over long periods and others, when grazing was reduced for some reason, when there was a surge of growth. Perhaps the biggest problem for the future is the risk of modern management ironing out the ups and downs of the past, the rather controlling current view of the natural environment actually preventing natural processes because they are seen as both random and damaging.

There were a lot more problems. As hydraulic diggers became available after WW2, FC had carried out extensive drainage work. People rightly ask: 'how could this have happened?' It was another remit problem: amazingly, in the New Forest Acts the FC is required to 'drain the forest' for grazing. Dug-out drains were eroding upwards into the mires. Deputy Surveyor Arthur Barlow and I managed to scrape together £8,000 per annum from the existing budget and started building small concrete dams. It was lucky we didn't get too far.

In the meantime Jonathan Spencer and I were discussing the bigger picture and concluded that something much more fundamental was needed – that somewhere around 2,000 hectares of habitat should be restored. In the lead were the 'Verderers Enclosures', areas of heath planted in the 1950s as a mechanism to fund the

Forest Vision

Verderers through rent paid by FC. Heathland vegetation still thrived in these recent plantings which were generally blots on the landscape and, being on poorer soils than existing woodland, were often growing trees rather badly.

Engaged in the day-to-day battles of the forest, I realised it might be difficult for the Deputy Surveyor to make what could look like major concessions; so an interregnum between Arthur Barlow and his successor Donald Thompson was a good moment to float the big ideas. Once the proposals were on the table they grew and grew, eventually into a complete series of plans covering the whole of the FC-managed land of the New Forest and the FC's biggest, riskiest and most complex community engagement – probably the biggest of its type anywhere in rural England to date.

'New Forest New Future', as the project became known, deployed every approach learnt over the years into a complex communication and negotiation. Led by Donald Thompson, Mike Seddon, latterly Deputy Surveyor himself, and planning forester Bruce Rothnie played the key roles in the design and management of the process. At the heart was a forum bringing representatives of all the New Forest interests from conservation to sawmilling together round a table. Once broad principles – and that there would be extensive habitat restoration was key – were established FC produced draft plans which were then considered by the forum. The forum worked very hard indeed and the commitment of time and effort the members put in must be a fantastic exemplar of the 'Big Society' at work. For FC at the centre, we weren't as confident as we might have seemed. From the start we recognised it could all go horribly wrong and an inevitable crunch point came after I'd handed over chairmanship to James Swabey, who steered the process past the rocks with consummate skill, and with his heart in his mouth.

FC set out to talk to everyone. First, we started reporting through a Stewardship report to every household in the New Forest, and followed it up with regular reports on the process. We set

Chapter 8: The New Forest

up 'drop-in' exhibitions at public libraries and, what proved most popular and effective, had walks to view the plans on the ground. The one technique put on the back burner was the traditional indoor public meeting because experience told us they tended to become platforms for the noisiest and most extreme views.

FC did not, however, go it alone: in talking to the wider community we worked with our partners who were brave enough to come out on the walks, explain their point of view and absorb some of the flack. By far the most contentious issue was heathland restoration along the 'Waterside', facing Southampton. Local people objected strongly to the removal of the Corsican Pine 'buffer' between the Forest and their villages because they valued the shelter for dog walking and, as with a lot of heathland restoration, just did not want change. The conservationists on the forum, against my advice, insisted on putting out plans showing the 100-year ambition for restoration when the much-less alarming 25-year plan would have done as well – as I predicted, we ended up with people objecting to plans projected for well beyond any of our lifetimes. Ironically, in view of what happened in 2011, the conservationist's rationale was that they wanted something in place to which they could hold FC! Had FC been abolished and its land passed on to someone else, all this and many other plans would probably have fallen – or at the very least become the subject of some very expensive bids for government funding. The debate resulted in a good compromise; this has already seen extensive heathland restoration. The big difference this time round was that we had all heard the arguments and agreed together, rather than FC being caught between two opposing views and reaching the 'wrong' decision for both.

The problem of presentation was critical and this is where the other key player, landscape architect Roger Worthington, comes in. Roger drew the new designs and has in fact probably designed a larger area of England's landscape than anyone alive today. Roger and I had been concerned about the 'user friendliness' of FC plans. Thanks to Sylvia Crowe, the FC's first, and inspirational, landscape consultant, plans were at least presented in perspective, as you see the land from the ground, rather than as flat maps which only expert map readers could decipher. However, they were designed for professionals – felling areas portrayed in primary colours – and were very hard for the non-expert to make much sense of. When we tried to introduce computer-generated trees they were ghastly artificial cones and lollipops! Roger experimented with a range of approaches, initially hand-drawn trees and vegetation, but later, as computer programmes developed, he lifted photos of habitat and superimposed them to show change – so where trees were to be removed for heathland, he could 'stick' heathland photos over the relevant area. Oblique air photos, taken specially from a light plane to look down towards an area of land as if from a viewpoint, were the other thing that worked very well.

I was particularly pleased with the nature conservation input to the whole process. Russell Wright for English Nature held his corner firmly, but without the intransigence and inflexibility that could have antagonised local participants. He probably won far more as a result, because I think many of the people round the table started to understand and sympathise with the conservation view, and to link it to their own and the Forest's heritage in a way they hadn't done before. RSPB have traditionally had a limited role in the Forest, still true today, but Regional Conservation Officer Chris Corrigan's input was the exception, hugely valuable and a very important player in keeping the process on track. My regret, which maybe can start to be rectified, is that the experience and lessons of New Forest New Future do not seem to have registered more widely with RSPB or Natural England at a corporate level – and there are challenges ahead which need that expertise and learning, especially if heathland ambitions are to have any prospect of success.

The New Forest, its communities and the FC, ended up getting far more from New Forest New Future than could ever have been hoped for. The depth of knowledge brought to bear on the plans was staggering: I remember a day with several commoners

Chapter 8: The New Forest

hunched over a plan debating where a traditional 'drift' (a gap between timber enclosures for moving stock) had run in their fathers' day. We were literally putting the heritage of the forest back in place. FC had traditionally been the punch bag between the different interests, often seen to be favouring the 'opposition'.

For FC the forum was a lightening rod: interests could argue face to face, with FC doing its job as neutral chair. That has been a lasting benefit. It's true FC had been defensive and sometimes secretive: the high-pressure politics of the Forest made it seem necessary, but also foresters hadn't liked to have their decisions questioned. The openness of New Forest New Future, and the FC's new ability to listen, massively increased trust between FC and its key partners. FC also gained confidence in what could be achieved – and how open it could be to other people's ideas.

That was all very well, but what about the money? The £8,000 per annum Arthur Barlow and I managed to free from the maintenance budget was not going to go far. In fact, the solution was already in place because, following the ESSO sponsorship we'd already gone on to win European LIFE funding – the first of three programmes. New Forest Operations Manager Alison Field, through meticulous, painstaking work, which challenged many of the FC's stuffy accounting practices, had managed to 'match up' virtually the whole £800,000 annual open forest budget into a stunning restoration programme. Our £8,000 grew into over £1 million invested in the bogs. Restoration started with research which showed our crude early approach would have been a disaster – blocking off the flow with a dam wasn't the answer, as water flowed through these systems throughout the profile. The answer was a permeable means to slow flow, and therefore siltation, and to block all the drains dug through the mires. Heather bales were the convenient solution, the material for them cut from nearby. Literally thousands and thousands went into the drains over the next few years.

The eventual plans came to a little over 2,000 hectares of habitat restoration, half of it heathland, much already completed by

2011. Some of the sharpest, most unnatural plantation edges were lost in the process. The vegetation of existing heathland was generally in pretty good condition at this point, but erosion on the fragile sandy soils was a real problem and significant funding and effort went to containing it.

Some Oak plantations are also being converted towards an A&O structure: they will be opened up to grazing and are being heavily thinned to allow big, open-crowned trees to develop, and also to create glades.

The final phase of the EU LIFE projects was particularly exciting: based around the Forest's watercourses, it put the meanders back in rivers straightened out in the drainage phase after the war. The results were immediate and spectacular: slowed by the old winding course water that would have rushed to the sea (contributing to flooding in Lymington on the way) backed up and spread amongst the trees.

The Environment Agency, who were partners in the project, allowed the experiment in the New Forest because there were no houses it could harm: it begs the question of just how much could be done more widely to buffer flooding, and generate resilience against climate change by extensive use of land to store and manage peak flows: far more than can ever be achieved pouring more and more concrete, and potentially far cheaper.

FC's role had changed: no longer was there even a pretence that in the New Forest its main aim was timber production so Deputy Surveyor Donald Thompson approached our supportive and knowledgeable Minister, Elliot Morley, who commissioned a review of the mandate. Signed by Secretary of State, Nick Brown, the mandate ordered the FC's priorities as:

- Conservation of the Natural and Cultural Heritage
- Public Enjoyment
- Rural Development (including timber production)

And in that order.

Chapter 8: The New Forest

The Minister charged the FC with 'continuing to maintain extensive local consultations'.

FC as a whole needs a new remit. It can be done. The New Forest, most important of all the National Forests in England, has already blazed the trail.

Demonstrating the new confidence, Desmond Swayne's (Conservative, New Forest West) contribution to the parliamentary debate in 2011 was warming: 'we don't want interference from Edinburgh (FC GB HQ)' he thundered 'we want local governance'. So far, so good – right on message – but then he left the pitch completely 'and we want the Forestry Commission to manage' – a real compliment; but actually a very serious message, because I believe the FC has achieved what many politicians and civil servants would see as the impossible: a national, central Government body deploying all the skill and power its scale gives it to a very special, complex local agenda.

Chapter 9

Organisation and Management

Set up in 1919 as a 'Commission', FC started with a largely non-executive board selected mainly from the private landowners who had lobbied for its creation. Over the years the board changed, with more executive Commissioners and a constitution that required seats to be filled by, for example, a timber processor, a trade union representative and, later, a representative of the environment sector. Whilst ministers did have the final say, the sectors were able to put forward their nominations. This system worked remarkably well in preventing the board becoming overtly political. The Chairman was generally political and a member of the party of the government in power, so valuable in maintaining links to the political establishment. Occasional attempts to introduce a political slant through ministerial appointments had little impact. With devolution in the late 1990s there was a need for even representation of each of the three countries so this system broke down and appointments are now made through the public appointments system. Apart from the fact that there is not the moderating influence of nominations from the sectors there is now a further problem: the rise of the career 'quangocrats', whose income depends in part on public appointments. Future appointments depend most heavily – and with limited transparency – on civil servants rather more than ministers and there is a very real pressure not to rock the boat – largely neutralising the raison d'être of non-executives on boards.

The FC was a Great Britain organisation – Northern Ireland has a separate Forest Service but over the last decade the countries

Chapter 9: Organisation and Management

have become more and more important, culminating in the absorption of FC in Wales into the single body Natural Resources Wales which now covers water, nature conservation, landscape and access and forestry.

Today the FC tells people that it is a 'non-ministerial government department' but everyone knows it as a 'quango'.

The FC has two principal functions: as a direct land manager of the national forests and as the regulator, and grant and advice giver, for the whole forestry sector. Its third function is forest research, through its research agency.

By the time I joined in 1976 the original country directorates had disappeared and FC had just moved its headquarters from London and Basingstoke to Edinburgh. It was organised into conservancies (effectively regions), districts and forests. Conservancies performed the dual function of land management and regulation. The organisation was divided very firmly into classes: graduate District Officers, Foresters holding a forester's certificate or more-modern equivalent and practical forest workers. The class divide started to break down with the class-to-class promotion of foresters to District Officer grades. The class system continued to evolve until eventually the organisation had a 'unified workforce' where anyone sufficiently qualified or skilled could move up the organisation. Later, higher grades joined the unified Civil Service, but when I joined all qualified foresters were classed as 'Professional and Technology Officers', rather than generalist civil servants. FC remains one of the very few bodies run at the very top by people with a specialist qualification in the organisation's field.

The organisation changed with pressures for economy and better communications: the original forest boundaries were drawn when most people went to work on a bike. 'Forests' and 'Districts' were amalgamated into 'Forest Districts' with specialists harvesting, forest management and recreation and environment staff, rather than the previous geographical approach and in 1985 the number of conservancies was reduced.

A bigger change came in 1992 when, as a fallout from the 'Flow Country', the organisation was split between the land management and regulatory functions – the land management became Forest Enterprise, and regulation and grants became Forestry Authority. In England the split was made by reducing the land management areas from three to two, north and east run from York, south and west from Bristol and the Authority arm from the third office in Cambridge. Roger Busby and I added further to the confusion by refusing to change the forest signs in south and west from Forestry Commission to Forest Enterprise because there had been no real effort to advertise the switch in name. We considered that Forestry Commission was a valuable brand in both commercial and political terms. It may have been partly our fault, but public recognition of the Forest Enterprise name never rose much above 10% whilst Forestry Commission achieved 70%. Forest Enterprise wasn't helped by the media quickly dubbing it 'the commercial arm of the Forestry Commission'.

We were continually amalgamating districts until they ended up close to the size of the conservancies in the 1970s. The two English regions were then joined into Forest Enterprise England, and not long after devolution struck, and the emphasis fell back on countries, with the dormant country committees revived, and the regulatory head promoted to country director and Forestry Commissioner level. Devolution did make a real difference because the money rested with each country and FC England's real axis became with Defra in London rather than FC's Great Britain Edinburgh HQ.

There is a fundamental problem at the heart of FC's existence which has caused more and more trouble as time has gone on. Government recognises only three sorts of organisation: spending departments, which spend money to provide services; money raising departments, principally the taxation bodies now one in Her Majesty's Revenue and Customs; and public businesses, most created during the nationalisation era after WW2 and now largely returned to the private sector. A spending department like Natural

Chapter 9: Organisation and Management

England is quite simple: there are tasks to carry out and grants to dispense, and there is a simple settlement between the government department and the Treasury. The department will always want to spend more, the Treasury less. The problem with FC is that it operates as both a business and as a spending department: timber should pay for itself but managing forest walks and restoring wildlife habitat fall firmly into spending department territory. The problem is compounded by the fact that a large proportion of environmental work is delivered as part of forestry operations, which vastly reduces costs compared to the same work delivered as a grant-funded conservation project. But what at one level is a saving on government spending can at another be seen as an excess cost on a timber business.

It's all quite complex and FC's accounts don't help: they are complex even by government standards. Additionally, as FC changes on the ground, its remit and financing have simply not kept up. It is not altogether the fault of current ministers that they started out seeing FC as mainly about timber, and therefore a business with no place in the public sector: were FC just that it would be hard, verging on impossible, to argue for public-sector land ownership. In an era of inflated bullshit FC must be almost unique in having run way beyond its own remit and propaganda (if you can call FC's feeble national communication that). It is far more modern, far more relevant, and far more plugged into its citizen supporters than anything you'll find in official reports – or even in most of its own informal publicity. I have to admit that, over the years, I kept having to create policy for what we'd just done – the one saving grace being that you can't lose when you've already succeeded. A strange beast for anyone to deal with.

The Forestry Commission does not think about management much. Every now and again there is a re-organisation, usually to economise on staffing, but management fads don't tend to penetrate. Being interested in these things, I found it frustrating at times but also an asset in terms of being able to evolve through prods and tweaks rather than through fashionable lurches. Just how much time do they absorb in most businesses?

The FC I joined was typically hierarchical. Because it is run by foresters from top to bottom it is, however, very cohesive: there is a common understanding of both practice and motivation.

After 1988, in England a remarkable process accelerated over two decades. Forest Enterprise, the land managers, became more and more outcome focussed – a reflection of the characters and approach of the people involved. Traditional management structures, especially in the public sector, impose a series of hurdles for people at the bottom of the heap to jump if they want to develop new ideas. The senior management, keen to protect their backs, then jump on any failures. Gradually, without really thinking about it, the England senior management turned the normal approach on its head: it got to the point of hunting the next project, ready to jump on new ideas developed locally, such as Go Ape, and run hard with them nationally. At the same time, in pursuit of the goals, national managers increasingly became supporters of the people on the ground, working to give them the resources they needed and jumping in to help when things went wrong. As confidence grew, the empowerment of local managers to make decisions became greater and greater and the management structure genuinely flatter, as everyone worked together in their particular roles for a common goal.

Time and time again we said 'yes' when the rational self-protecting answer should have been 'no'. Each time we said 'yes' and succeeded the organisation became more dynamic, and the projects and ideas got bigger and more exciting.

Chief Executive Geoff Hatfield had a big influence: tenacious in pursuing a deal, he combined confidence and calm and in particular, an ability to tackle problems without personalising them: when things went wrong we dealt with them, but without getting excited and taking against managers who might have made a mistake. People knew they could take decisions without the fear of an attack, and more correct decisions resulted.

Chapter 9: Organisation and Management

It took confident management to let go to this extent, and also to push ever further into new territory. FC has a unique base in large-scale management: all the senior management had been managing land holdings of 20,000 hectares upwards for at least 20 years, and the Chief Executive manages more land – 260,000 hectares (600,000 acres) – than anyone else in England. For me there was a flip side: unlike some colleagues I never suffered from the illusion that FC had a God-given right to exist. The baseline in 1988 was very low indeed: forestry, and FC, had simply lost public confidence and support. FC was living on borrowed time and it needed to change, and to do it fast; to innovate and to deliver to have a place in the future. Whenever senior managers faced the question 'hold or go forward' the decision had always to be to go forward. We were constantly seeking the opportunity, the new idea, and most importantly, the contemporary direction as with the peri-urban programme.

Virtually every major project hit a bump at one time or another, and I imagine many organisations don't get over those bumps and then become even more risk averse.

A key effect of this approach was its impact on FC's local and regional approach: quite intentionally, the national often disappeared into the background. The support and leadership from the national level would only be apparent to the FC staff involved, with national managers very rarely appearing in public on projects. For example, the programme that became 'Newlands' (the regeneration of damaged land in the northwest) began nationally and has been supported nationally throughout but has an entirely northwest public identity. This is how it should be – with the one caveat that it is vital to understand how it works if you are trying to judge or change it. The national involvement was vital in providing perspective and scale as well as national-level expertise.

Two key factors contributed to the reliability of FC delivery. The first, dating back to 1989 was multi-skilled project teams. In the FC I joined, the Senior Forest Officer, in line with traditional authoritarian management, was deemed to know more about everything than his juniors did so you had the wonderful spectacle of a forestry-trained District Officer designing shop fittings. Gradually that changed: through project teams people were respected for their expertise, so professional designers were not casually overridden because they were junior. Similarly, in the FC I joined administrators were not always treated with respect by foresters, but people such as the Finance Officer became a crucial and respected equal in delivering the goods. As Chief Executive I spent far more time over spreadsheets with Steve Meeks, the excellent Head of Finance, than I did on the ground at project sites. With no financial slack, thanks to plummeting timber prices, we had to master the skills of EU cash flow and, running the sort of projects where other public bodies overrun by millions, we brought budgets in to a fraction of 1% year after year.

It got to the point where some of us stuffy, conventional foresters had to suspend our disbelief: when our Chief Designer Katrina Jeffries 'went purple' to make our leaflets more exciting and contemporary, some of us had to step back and accept we'd never quite get there but that the organisation had to be in tune with our visitors, not the tiny, unrepresentative minority that professional foresters are.

The other thing that helped a lot – a simple, transferable lesson – was an increasing suite of standard designs and practices, tree-planting specifications, recreation furniture, path construction, public-consultation approaches and even management of outdoor art, which managers could pull off the shelf and apply. It meant mistakes were not repeated and there was more time and energy to build the new and original because so many of the basics were taken care of. Simple, consistent, application of designer-led artefacts, such as sign structures and furniture, would do a huge amount to make the countryside more attractive, less cluttered and less urban.

What sets FC apart amongst countryside agencies and charities was the drive for continuous improvement. There is a common view amongst countryside providers that 'if it ain't broke don't fix

Chapter 9: Organisation and Management

it' – but how many of them are driving around in a Mark 1 Ford Escort, the era of the original A- frame picnic table? Already some of the young workers who installed the early A-frames when they were in their 20s must be getting old and a bit creaky – and will be finding just how difficult it is to slide in and out of a design that should have been improved, not still in constant use. With no illusions that everything was OK, FC was hungry to do better and scavenged remorselessly for the best of what others were doing. Often complacent because they know they are good and in the right, others in the same field have been slow to learn as FC provision has caught up and then pulled ahead in a wide range of fields.

At the height of FC's external-funding drive we achieved £15m per annum in third-party funding, more than the far-bigger Natural England and the Environment Agency. It was roughly 25% of total income and was delivered with the same level of senior staffing at national and district level, representing a huge productivity increase. It was 'competitive' funding; others could as easily have grabbed it had they been up for it. As time went on more and more of the money was aimed at wider, usually private sector, economic and social, benefits: sometimes, as at Dalby, direct on-site employment in small businesses, and sometimes more indirect – but probably bigger – underlying environmental improvement flashing back into economic development, as in the urban northwest.

So is it just being wise after the event? I have always been interested in how decisions are taken and implemented – rarely in the neat way the management textbooks suggest. Searching around in the files I found three papers from 2003, an article on charging in recreation for the United Nations *Sylva* magazine, a paper on community engagement given at an EU INTEREG conference in Paris, and a cross-cutting paper about FC's activities in the English national parks. If anything, they show our ideas were more clearly developed at the time than I had realised writing a decade later.

As I moved into national policy one last issue became very important: the relationship between specialists and generalists in the

Civil Service. It is an issue that has since grown to a degree of importance I could never have anticipated, as the Government and its supporting civil servants have struggled in public, caught out time and again during the current forestry debate, because FC expertise was cut out of the policy-making loop. I joined the Civil Service just after Harold Wilson's Fulton Commission had recommended a more professional Civil Service, with a higher proportion of staff qualified vocationally, rather than with a general qualification as is the British tradition. They cited the US model where many more staff had applicable qualifications, albeit mostly lawyers.

If anything, the Civil Service saw the threat and responded by reducing, rather than increasing, the role of qualified specialists. The Forestry Commission remained almost unique in being run by people qualified in the discipline within which it worked. The recent rash of external appointments of senior staff skilled in 'management' has further developed this in bodies such as Natural England and some of the big Non Governmental Organisations, with mixed success.

There is logic behind the generalist Civil Service: there is no doubt whatsoever that specialists argue for their own field and most FC staff see keeping the FC alive as a key part of their role. Applied generally, that clearly is not good for objective allocation of national resources. However, as recent events have shown, it also is not easy for generalists simply to pick up subjects in which they have no knowledge and make good policy. I think this is becoming a serious, looming issue in Defra and the environmental field. From 1947 on the old Ministry of Agriculture, Fisheries and Food basically tweaked an agreed approach to land use in which agriculture dominated and policy meant the limited adjustment of rules within a defined set of principles.

It is not like that anymore. New challenges demand fine judgements on fundamental science. It almost certainly needs a completely new ways of doing things. That does not sit well with the gradual evolution inherent in a system where generalists collect

Chapter 9: Organisation and Management

information from a range of sectoral interests and then balance out a solution – an approach for which the generalist Civil Service is well equipped. However, what is needed now is a deep understanding both of the fundamental engineering and the control levers available to the practical manager. What scares me is that the complex, cutting-edge new approaches developed by the FC have become increasingly difficult to communicate: many key people just do not have sufficient technical background to understand.

Similarly, there is a fundamental gap in understanding between the different silos – nature conservation, low carbon economy, environmental protection, economic accelerators and quality of life. Trying to bring them together is very hard work indeed. It is exacerbated by a further issue: the increasing professionalism of politicians – more and more people who have done nothing else but politics – who know how to make policy but are weak at the interface between policy and delivery. It first hit me during the Foot and Mouth epidemic in 2001 and has been all too obvious during the flooding crisis as I write.

The next major threat to FC's future was, in fact, organisational, the review of Defra carried out by Lord Haskins to rationalise rural delivery. The key targets were always English Nature and the Countryside Agency, with the Rural Development Service thrown in for good measure. FC was on the sidelines but definitely in the picture. This review was different, and in some ways less predictable, because it was not essentially destructive. It genuinely sought more effective government delivery and there were precedents in Scotland and Wales where nature conservation and countryside access had been brought together.

The story goes that FC started off being seen by Defra as a bit of a nuisance, but why not chuck it in for neatness, the fewer strange agencies knocking about the better. This is where Lord Clark of Windermere came in. I do not really understand what politicians do. He might return the compliment and say that he is not quite sure what FC managers do, but either way there was mutual respect behind the incomprehension. Thanks to his hard work, FC's reputation grew as the Haskins process went on. The people who mattered realised this was an organisation that was really making things happen.

That was the first hill climbed, but there was a further blip ahead: it was suggested that actually FC's dynamic culture might positively benefit the birth of Natural England, bringing in a stream of practical delivery skills. This was not a stupid idea. However, my concern over many, many years has been that forestry is just so small, so few people, that if FC went then forestry as a policy area would simply disappear into the maw of a big, busy department such as Defra. My time working closely with Defra more than confirmed that view: I can honestly say that I never met anything but friendly interest from Defra colleagues, but frequently a degree of bemusement about this strange little organisation clinging onto their skirt tails.

The debate around Haskins also resulted in the clearest – and very generous – recognition of how the FC had changed when *the Guardian*, reviewing the organisations, involved said of the FC 'radically changed to become one of Britain's most environmentally conscious agencies.' A fantastic accolade which gave all of us in FC great satisfaction.

So we waited with baited breath for the announcement – and FC stayed independent. It was a good decision for FC because Natural England did not have an easy birth and is still shaking out. It is always difficult to weigh the problem of many competing agencies, each one with central services, chief executives, management boards and so on, against the span of control one organisation can reasonably take on. My perception is that Natural England has done as good a job as it reasonably could, its focus developing primarily on the vital agri-environment grants. I have been involved around the Higher Level Stewardship Scheme and would strongly endorse NE's running of it; it is imaginative, not just process driven, a real partnership with landowners which is increasingly

Chapter 9: Organisation and Management

looking for results for wildlife and the landscape. The ex-Countryside Commission people side of the organisation has not gone so well; mixing the cultures is a struggle and the Countryside Commission input is a shadow of its 1980s zenith. I do think FC would have disappeared into this far-flung behemoth of an organisation, possibly without so much as a ripple.

Another reflection, bearing in mind current developments: FC has always been dominated by the land-management arm, with regulation and grants subsidiary. In contrast, English Nature and its predecessors were dominated by science, regulation and working with landowners. The practical management of the National Nature Reserves was always the junior partner, and inevitably the people overseeing them were unlikely to be selected for direct land management skills.

On top of FC's survival as an organisation, Haskins was important because it raised FC's profile as a deliverer, and FC was treated with growing respect in supporting Defra to deliver programmes such as the SSSI target.

Chapter 10

The Cutting Edge

Foot and Mouth disease struck on a snowy Monday in February 2001. Two days later, along with every other rural landowner, the Forestry Commission closed its entire estate in England. It stayed closed till May. Responding to the disaster, it was the catalyst for the Forestry Commission to develop even more radical solutions and move firmly into the forefront of rural development – and the rescue of derelict landscapes around our towns and cities.

The speed of the epidemic caught out government as it leapfrogged from region to region. It moved much faster because of the huge increase in animal movements as both sheep and cattle were traded across the country. Donald Thompson ordered the animals off the New Forest heaths: the idea of Foot and Mouth getting into this huge unenclosed area was unthinkable and could have threatened the centuries-old commoning culture. Sadly, in the less-regulated Forest of Dean, the disease got into the commoners' sheep, and what may have been the largest single cull took place on a closed and fenced public road near Speech House in the centre of the Forest.

Thanks to the Department of the Environment's Head of Access, Susan Carter, I got involved in some of Defra's key meetings as the crisis unfolded. It was quite unnerving for a relatively junior civil servant on the fringes of Whitehall to find the Chief Secretary to the Treasury taking the next seat at a crisis meeting. Susan was a convert to the FC, coming from a traditionally negative late 1980s position to appreciate the changes the Commission had made and

Chapter 10: The Cutting Edge

in particular its capability to deliver. This was a situation that needed practical delivery, and I learned a much-bigger lesson watching civil servants pulling policy levers and at a complete loss when the situation on the ground failed to improve. Highlighted by the crisis, this is a bigger, wider and vital issue: in the recent report of the Climate Change Adaptation Panel the problem of good policies failing to connect with practical delivery was highlighted. Eventually the army were called in. I recognised their approach: they'd worked out the logistics, time, people, vehicles and so on almost before the policy people had stopped talking. The opposite to a policy department, like the FC the army were programmed to immediate action.

The countryside was eerily quiet. Susan Carter told me she had a feeling of how pent up and restricted people felt in our hometown, Bristol. Parks were fuller than usual. In the countryside the horror of slaughter was matched by the growing economic distress of the huge number of businesses dependent on countryside visitors. In the end, the cost to farming was £1 billion, much returned in Government compensation, but the cost to the wider rural economy at least double with no compensation.

In fact, the FC had a limited role as the crisis unfolded. It was when it started to recede that we became major players: how to re-open the countryside, with the farming community traumatised and terrified to take any risks at all? FC took a very clear lead, strongly supported by ministers from across several departments. We devised safety criteria around proximity of outbreaks and the last date any animals had been slaughtered. There was significant opposition and FC ran up against the reluctance of others to move: in one county that had not had any outbreaks at all, landowners on the county council flexed their normally hidden muscles and refused to reopen public rights of way, hampering our ability to open the 'open access' FC forest through which they ran!

In the New Forest business was lobbying for the forest to re-open, the commoners were against it. As Donald Thompson moved

Forest Vision

to re-open he reported to me that he'd been attacked by forest businesses for going too slowly, then the commoners for going too fast, in the same village hall just a few days apart 'it looks like I'm probably getting it about right' was his dry comment.

An extraordinary and exciting situation was developing in the Lake District, one of the worst-hit regions. After several years summering on Bassenthwaite Water, in the middle of the crisis, a pair of Ospreys settled to nest in an artificial eyrie built in the forest above the lake by FC and the Lake District National Park. These were England's first nesting Ospreys for a century. With RSPB we told the world they were there – but not the precise location. Gradually the point where we could re-open got closer. Dodd Wood, which is leased to the FC by the very-supportive Fryer-Spedding family, is a steep round-topped hill directly across the lake from the nest. It was eerily quiet, no people around, when I visited the Forest Craftsmen as they put the finishing touches to paths and a viewing point, and we all saw the birds through my telescope.

The Chief Executive of Allerdale District Council had been lobbying hard for business in the area, sending increasingly strong letters to FC and the Forestry Minister. Early on the beautiful May morning after the 2001 General Election District Manager Graeme Prest, mastermind of the Osprey operation, and I met him outside the Whinlatter visitor centre. He had been up all night as returning officer. We told him that not only would we re-open within days but that we had the biggest bit of news possible to get people back into the Lake District.

The plan for the day of the launch was for a press briefing with Forestry Minister, Elliot Morley, followed by the official opening to the public, but the news went out on morning television. Elliot arrived to a press scrum and a full car park: the public had not waited for FC's carefully thought through plans. It all worked out well, with Elliot, a very keen birder in his own right, helping visitors see the distant nest through the bank of telescopes at the viewpoint. The weekend following was pandemonium as everyone came to

Chapter 10: The Cutting Edge

see these stunning birds; and since then over one million people have visited Dodd Wood and the Whinlatter visitor centre.

Illustrating the pain rural people suffered, a new tenant had just taken over the Sawmill café at the base of Dodd Hill when the countryside was closed. Her new business stopped dead in its tracks and like many others she faced ruin. She was very pleased when she heard about the Ospreys – not a birder, she thought she might get a busy weekend out of it. It is great that more than a decade on the café is still running flat out through the Osprey season, refreshing visitors after the long climb – a thriving business employing lots of local people.

On a much-wider front, it was the recognition by local businesses of just how important the forest was to rural tourism that started a new phase in the Forestry Commission's recreation story. It took the crisis for a powerful new alliance between the public and private sectors to develop, and it was one that we in FC grasped with enthusiasm.

There was money for post Foot and Mouth regeneration and the northern Regional Development Agencies understood the link between environment and the economy. Cumbria rapidly came in with support for the Osprey project with funding to modernise the Whinlatter visitor centre, to support the Osprey project and provide a video link from the nest to the visitor centre. For the first two years the video link was on an ordinary TV screen in a Portakabin. So powerful were the close up images of the nest that noisy visitors to the hut were shushed by people watching so entranced they thought the Ospreys might be disturbed – the Ospreys were actually three miles away with a mountain in between! Both at the centre and up at the viewpoint staff and volunteers are there through the breeding season to help people see the Ospreys, and to tell them how nesting is going. Back at the centre the TV link, now giant flat screens, shows the growing young on the nest. Ospreys have become a symbol of the Lakes: perfect for projecting this pristine natural environment, centred around its glittering waters. Not,

Forest Vision

however, all as glittering as they might be: Bassenthwaite itself has a range of pollution and siltation problems and the Ospreys proved the catalyst for a major project to research and then solve them, cleaning up this iconic lake.

Two new ideas were developing in East Anglia, at the High Lodge visitor centre, thanks to the imagination of District Manager Jim Lyon and Recreation Manager Mike Taylor. They reflected FC's growing confidence that it could be a popular player in the countryside. First were the concerts, which grew and got local authority support as a great way to promote the region and were soon featuring big name bands from across the spectrum – each night pulling in a very different audience. Some bands us oldies had never heard of. Chief Executive Geoff Hatfield emailed that he 'was unable to comment on Atomic Kitten as none of my children are at home'.

The other new idea was Go Ape: walking in the treetops 50ft above the ground on single wires then zipping down to the ground or a catching net. Obviously a massive safety risk and not the sort of thing a risk-averse civil servant should go near. We took one look at it, realised it was inspired, and so dangerous that it had to be completely safe. The concerts became a tour and we gave Go Ape founder Crispin Mayhew a licence for as many forests as he wanted and a rent 'holiday' while he got set up. We did not repeat the Moors Valley Playtrail mistake again: these great ideas were spread as widely and as quickly as possible, all over England.

Both have succeeded spectacularly: concerts get people out into the forest who might never normally visit. Go Ape reminded me of the chef ranting 'I don't want my diners going away 'satisfied' I want them to have the best meal they've ever had'. No one left Go Ape 'satisfied' it was 'I've never been so scared in my life, never again' or I've never been so scared in my life, when can I go round again?'. It took a lot more than Go Ape's fail-safe harnesses to persuade people they weren't about to drop to a distant forest floor! Their comment books are incredible – normally, comment books

Chapter 10: The Cutting Edge

filled in by teenagers are full of silly comments and rude drawings. Not here: it's all heartfelt 'wows' and 'OMGs' ('Oh My God') about the sheer adrenaline-rushing thrill of the long zip wires, and the achievement of conquering the lethal stirrups. It's fun, but to me it's more than fun: like the kids gaining confidence at Moors Valley this is the sort of thrill and testing physical and mental challenge people just don't get in their super-safe modern lives. And what surroundings! Nothing could be further from the turn-off of the soulless, TV watching sweat, of an urban gym.

Whinlatter soon had its Go Ape, but Dalby was the first centre to have it built in from the planning stage. Thanks to National Park officer, Andy Wilson, and the support of the local business community, plans for a major new visitor centre went through and got funding, much of it again from EU regional development funds. A new build in a national park, the new centre went on to win a Prime Minister's award for Best Public Building of the year. It stood at the heart of a really fantastic place for people: stunning woods and everything from waterside strolls to brand-new custom-built mountain-bike trails and Go Ape: every sort of leisure, from the gentlest to the extreme. Dalby featured a very high proportion of private business under the FC 'umbrella' development, café, shop, cycle hire, sales and spares, meeting rooms, craft studios. I met District Manager Alan Eves, the Monday after the opening of the new development. 'Terrible' he said when I asked him how it had gone. 'Why ? What went wrong ?' 'They were queuing right out to the Scarborough road' Alan replied 'the parking filled up and we had to turn people away'. Dalby is an institution in North Yorkshire: that is how much people value their forests.

My overriding lesson from Foot and Mouth, however, is the vital importance of that link between policy and delivery. In FC delivery was taken for granted, and I learned a lot as I watched clever people struggling in what, to them, was foreign territory. Deliverers do not make much noise. They don't have time. Forget them at your peril. We are going to need FC's skill and versatility more and more

Forest Vision

as the shocks of changing climate pose governments bigger and bigger challenges.

The FC had been involved in research on damaged land for nearly 50 years by 1995. It had been applied on a large scale restoring the Welsh coalfields, run by a dedicated FC unit, but in England had never progressed beyond the experimental stage. I had been involved in two attempts to get greater involvement: with MAFF in the late 1980s and in the Black Country in the early 1990s.

To FC fury, it was the Countryside Commission riding high under the inspirational leadership of Chairman Derek Barber and Director-General Adrian Phillips, that came up with the idea of the English community forests and also the National Forest. Whilst the FC fought at GB level, in England we watched closely. England Director Tim Rollinson took it a step further in the first England Forestry Strategy, skilfully brokered across the main government organisations with an interest in forestry.

FC did, however, buy land in the community forests and in the National Forest, places such as Rosliston, a former dairy farm, now a thriving forest centre. Rosliston, like other early sites was planted with conifers and broadleaves; attractive mixed woodland with shelter and winter colour from the conifers. However, as time went on planting became more and more broadleaved. Rosliston was followed by Nightingale Wood in the Swindon community forest, Overscourt in the Forest of Avon and many, many more woods in most of the community forests over the following years.

New planting caused problems again. Working on poor, upland soils, foresters had learnt always to plough. However, on fertile ex-farmland weeds grew on a truly heroic scale. We should have known better: I had seen early farm woodlands, and planting into unploughed fallow with a light cover of self sown 'volunteer' wheat or Barley from the last crop, proved very successful. But the lesson was learned and subsequent planting on agricultural land has used a special sowing of slow-growing grasses with trees planted into bare patches made with herbicide.

Chapter 10: The Cutting Edge

The real breakthrough came in the Nottinghamshire coalfield in a deal between FC, led by Regional Director Geoff Hatfield and District Manager John Tewson, and Nottinghamshire County Council, to restore 800 hectares to woodland. This was in the aftermath of the collapse of the coal industry and there was serious money going into regenerating communities and improving their environment. It was a huge opportunity that FC grasped with enthusiasm. Vast black mountains, the coal tips started with a settling lagoon on top that had to be filled in. In a last twitch of traditional forestry the GB headquarters in Scotland insisted that the project be justified on forestry economic grounds, completely missing the point, and leaving a strange relict of extensive Corsican Pine. The settling ponds surrounding the tips were turned into attractive ponds for fishing and birds, whilst shallower pools, adjoining wet grassland and even concrete hard standing were habitat for waders including Little Ringed Plovers.

The Nottinghamshire coalfield took FC into the strange, twilight world of the urban fringe. It is the world of *Edgelands*. In it, the authors describe the informal, damaged landscapes of mineral workings, self-sown woodlands, hidden, unnamed ponds, scrap yards and fly tipping. Calling it 'England's true wilderness', they have a point: this is land on people's doorsteps, a secret world for generations of children, a place of unexpected horrors and delights for adults. For me it is epitomised by a flock of Avocets wheeling in evening sunshine over RSPB's Cliffe Marshes reserve, a grubby dredger passing on the Thames behind; and perhaps by a Little Egret fishing on Rainham Marshes, spotted from a speeding Eurostar. At their worst, the 'Edgelands' can be pretty awful places to live: it was a revelation to find people living with a 200ft black coal tip as their view, or a landfill site at the bottom of the garden, just a 10ft high earth mound between them and the smell, the dust, and the noise of delivery lorries and excavators spreading the detritus. I had a powerful sense that what we did next could be the factor that tipped a residential area into prosperity or decay.

Forest Vision

The 'Edgelands' are as much a political as a physical no man's land. Many are in the Green Belt. The original Green Belt policy was an act of inspiration, and is even more important today as planning relaxation hits the political agenda. But the Green Belt is basically a negative tool: it stops things happening, except for 'permitted development' ranging from cemeteries to landfill sites which at its worst can turn the edges of our towns into a scene of dereliction. Within central government the urban department – the Department of Environment, Transport and the Regions (DETR), then John Prescott's Office of the Deputy Prime Minister (ODPM), now the Department for Communities and Local Government (DCLG) – holds sway but does not understand the rural. All powerful in the countryside, the agriculture department MAFF, now Defra, recognises the power of its bigger brother and keeps well clear. Compounding the problem is hope value (speculative land purchase in the expectation of hitting the planning jackpot). It is a particularly serious blot because the last thing the speculator wants is anything to detract from the land's development potential; so, absolutely no trees, and a bit of illegal fly tipping is certainly welcome, to create an environment where development would be a merciful release.

Reclaiming England's derelict land has been problematical and the landscape is scattered with failures. Because urban practitioners often have no idea at all about rural land management, their solutions, egged on by landscape architects on percentage fees, have often been unnecessarily expensive and inappropriate: hugely expensive tree planting with 4-metre tall urban trees, trickle irrigation piping water to each individual tree, bark mulch and so on adding up to astronomic bills. Equally awful is the planners' urban park solution: acres of bleak mown grass, ghastly 'best-value' woods with hard edges, regular shapes, and the ubiquitous red-berried non-native shrubs. And, of course, there is always the pond with the island, so steep sided that only Canada Geese and Coots can use it. In the coalfields the countryside is littered with half-hearted reclamation – surviving trees barely growing, and a decaying sign

Chapter 10: The Cutting Edge

trumpeting a 15-year-old project: the only remnant of a quick fix. Cheap at the time – expensive as a failure. FC inherited a lot of reclamation design. Superficially it looked great on paper: but who came up with the idea of reflecting the local field pattern on a huge mound which bore no relation to the surrounding landscape? Fundamental errors were as simple as paths planned up slopes so steep that they were certain to wash away in the first serious storm.

Forest Research, the driver of re-forestation had, by the late 1990s, become rather detached from its traditional delivery-based focus, not helped by an incompetent attempt to 'marketise' its relationship with practical foresters. However, Andy Moffat's Soils and Reclamations team became the exemplar of a return to close working between practical foresters and researchers. Faced with an amazing range of damaged sites their science was what got the trees to grow, and they became popular within research because Forest Enterprise was paying – for once there was the money to hire them.

There is some really good work in the private sector, too: a few years ago, for example, I visited several sites by Banks Mining, well designed and executed right down to a beautifully sculpted 'natural landform'. That site, however, looked out over a classic failing, half-hearted, planting (Not by Banks!) on the old coal tip opposite. Some of the partnership gravel pit restoration along river valleys where mineral companies and conservationists are working together are producing stunning new wetlands. However, even the best company's business is minerals, not land management, and successor managers to take the land over, as well as the money to fund them, are essential.

The next two targets were the Thames Gateway and the North West, the Manchester-Liverpool conurbation. District Manager Sandy Greig, Project Forester Joe Watts and Thames Chase Community Forest Head John Meehan produced a plan in Thames Chase Community Forest on London's eastern boundary, identifying potential land that might become available for woodland. In the North West I met Tom Ferguson of St Helen's Borough and Richard

Sharland of Groundwork St Helens, to discuss a role for FC in taking forward their ground-breaking 'Wasteland to Woodlands' programme. We stood on top of Sutton Manor colliery, a 200ft-high blackened waste, and down below several of the houses facing this depressing view were boarded up. That day, as we agreed to take over the restoration, I decided the real test would be what happened to those houses – new windows, new people moving in? Or demolished like so many houses in the North West? With these opportunities, FC set up a land regeneration unit headed by Chris Robinson, and shortly afterwards the breakthrough came: in 2000 the Treasury granted the FC £10 million under the Capital Modernisation Fund (CMF), brokered by Alan Stevenson for FC, for the two areas, and ushered in a decade of spectacular development.

The timescale was very short: two years, later extended to three. We looked at the critical path and realised getting hold of the land was the key issue; thanks to Geoff Hatfield's decisive leadership we were advertising for land agents just two weeks after the money was granted. Planning the new woods was key and from the start everyone was clear these were for people first; timber and other objectives second. These were woods, not plantations, and open space was as important as trees. Over the programme as a whole the area planted with trees came out at just 50%; open ground included very wide rides to ensure people were able to feel safe and not closed in by the trees, areas identified as of conservation importance, and some sites where there was so much of the best of the Edgelands they did not need changing. Bob McIntosh, very supportive as Chief Executive, did nearly give up on us when we took him to one site, trashed by heavy industry to leave an incredible complex of self-sown trees, pools, and reedbeds, and explained we only intended to actually plant 2 of the 20 hectares!

Access was everything, and the path construction developed all those years ago in the Forest of Dean really came into play. CMF funding constructed over 70km of new wheelchair-quality paths. Engineers can be a problem: they like straight lines and it could be

Chapter 10: The Cutting Edge

difficult to persuade them these were not forest roads. Mike Hough, Civil Engineer for Thames Chase, excelled: his passion for the exact right surface for smooth-running wheelchairs matched mine and he took no persuading to plan every path with the landscape architect, beautiful paths snaking between the trees, looking so effortless that visitors could never imagine how much work had gone into getting them just right. Our chunky furniture design was critical too: vandalism was expected to be a serious problem on some sites. However, we increasingly put people at the core of the programme. CMF coincided with a concerted drive to engage forest communities. James Swabey and David Thorpe did a nationwide 'roadshow' to tell FC staff it was fine to talk to the public. At Viridor Wood, an early site, Chris Robinson and I agonised over vandalism. There was a fishing pond. The ex-miners fishing there were big blokes. We built them another pond. There was no vandalism. People's response varied: in the Notts coalfield an FC van was bombarded with stones; at the other end of the spectrum, Chris himself on an inspection visit was threatened by youths who thought he was going to damage their trees.

As the Notts coalfield work came to an end, FC moved on to south Yorkshire and a new suite of similar coalfield sites.

These became exciting woods because of the suggestions people made, and they were the woods people wanted. At Pages Farm, in Thames Chase, a stunning sweep of Oxeye daisies was suggested by local kids to go under a power line where trees could not be planted. It is next to the specially surfaced horse-riding trail. My favourite of all – is it unique, I wonder? – is the dog swimming pond at Jeskyns Wood. Art and activity have played a big part. Possibly my favourite site of all is Ingrebourne Hill, on the very edge of east London. It is favourite because it was so awful when I first saw it. Admittedly, it was only an inert waste landfill – construction rubble, not household waste – but it was still smelly. All that separated it from the hundreds of people living in adjacent houses was a 10ft-high earth bund. A primary school stuck out on a promontory into the middle of the landfill. Today, it really is a doorstep wood. From Avalon Road you can walk straight off the street into the wood. Now those same people look out onto growing trees, very successful wildflower meadows, shallow-sided, wildlife rich pools and stacks of activity for kids and adults: a fibreglass climbing rock, a dipping, winding mountain-bike activity course, and a network of paths for everything from bikes to wheelchairs. What really pleases me is the number of children and teenagers out on the site: experience shows that real life can drag them away from the computer screen. Why shouldn't everyone have an Ingrebourne Hill on their doorstep? And why shouldn't everyone have the sort of childhood adventure described in *Edgelands* (if a little bit more health and safety conscious!)?

CMF concluded in a carefully planned panic: we built more paths in the last quarter of the project than ever before in FC. The project's Treasury sponsor visited Thames Chase and floored me when she asked: 'How did you do so much in so little time?'. Friendly questions from the Treasury are not a big part of FC history! In the clash between reality and politics, we had realised from the first how tight the timing was. Almost forgotten in the political blame game, the government achieved a huge amount at this time through its re-investment in the nation but the mistake was not warming up deliverers beforehand – more time for planning before the money came on stream would have made a big difference. For FC it was a spectacular demonstration of its delivery ability, technical skill and flexibility – especially in developing its community engagement: a scary and unfamiliar area of work. Other CMF projects struggled and even failed to get off the ground at all. A lot of CCTV cameras went up and whether they achieved the aim of trialling new approaches for wider application I cannot comment, but for peri-urban forestry CMF worked spectacularly.

Even while the programme was rolling Martin Reynolds of the North West Regional Development Agency (NWRDA) had put in a further £1 million. With the two community forests, and particularly

Chapter 10: The Cutting Edge

Mersey Forest Director Paul Nolan, a critical player in everything that has been achieved in the North West, a much bigger programme was developed and the £50 million 'Newlands' came into being, aimed at cracking some of the hardest nuts in the North West: the RDA was faced with a range of restoration sites they just could not shift and FC soon realised why they were so difficult: most were in multiple ownership, most in multiply deprived communities and in some cases it proved impossible to find who really owned the land!

One of the problems facing environmental improvement is that the economics driving evidence-based decision-making struggles with a lot of the things that go to make up 'liveability'. Everyone laughed at David Cameron's 'Happiness' index but it is a really serious issue: whatever the Ad men would like us to believe, for most people there is more to life than shopping. NWRDA didn't commit £50m just because they were nice guys. Their globe-trotting business salesmen reported back that international companies saw England's North West as a derelict post-industrial landscape – not the sort of place in which they wanted to invest. Nowhere was that better illustrated than on an early Newlands site, Mostyn Vale, with a huge new Fujitsu complex on one side of the very tatty site, and a declining estate with boarded up houses and a rough reputation on the other. For the RDA this project was about hard economics: improving the region's image in parallel with making better places for people to live.

It is worth mentioning a key driver in all of this: cost. FC was spending money on a scale it hadn't experienced since the heady days of upland land acquisition. For many sites, there was funding to do pretty much anything people asked for. It was a bonanza, we could let our imaginations rip. For the funders, however, it was orders of magnitude cheaper than they expected, and they were amazed at what they got for their money: the secret, the rural/urban divide and the intensity of operations between an urban park and a much bigger, less intensively invested peri-urban woodland. I reckon that a peri-urban wood costs 5-10 times less to establish and manage than an urban park – but also 5-10 times more than a deep rural forest.

The scene in the Thames Gateway was more confused with perhaps 60 bodies competing for attention. Where did FC go next? It was hard to see a rather retiring organisation with no marketing ability competing with all the glitz and political pull of our competitors. We need not have worried. The brilliant head of the Thames Gateway Delivery Unit, Mittesh Dhanak, was looking for action and getting very frustrated with endless reports that led nowhere. Once again – the gap between policy and delivery. He saw what FC had achieved and solved our problem by coming straight to us. FC was ready, but not quite for what came next: not long before the 2005 election was called he rang up and asked whether FC could do him a conservation project between £1 and £2 million? Fine so far, but the sting was the timescale: in four weeks. It was impossible but I said yes anyway. Ten days later a farm came on the market right next to Gravesend, a key Gateway target. Twelve days later FC bought it and a couple of weeks after that Tony Blair and John Prescott sailed down the Thames and announced the purchase on Gravesend Pier. Jeskyns came as part of a wider package – there was money for Ingrebourne, too.

OK, it was an election stunt; but of all the election stunts over the years this is one that has a chance to last, and far longer than any of us could imagine today. Look at the Royal Parks: there has to be a very good chance Jeskyns Wood will still be there in 200 years' time. Not that it was an easy birth: Jeskyns is right on the divide between the 'haves' and the 'have nots' – the deprived Medway towns on the coast and the wealthy commuter belt of rural Kent. The 'haves' did not like it. By now spending more on recreation infrastructure than on trees was normal. At Jeskyns the public consultation alone cost more than the trees. Once again, trees, or at least forest trees, do not dominate, with a design that aims to take this ex-oilseed rape field back towards something more like the

Chapter 10: The Cutting Edge

Kent of the old days, with flower-rich meadows and orchards as well as lots for kids to do and, of course, that dog swimming pond.

The purchase of Jeskyns was signed off personally by John Prescott who was a very active supporter of what FC was doing, visiting sites in the North West several times. Immensely to his credit, I do not see it as particularly politically slanted. After all, it was Michael Heseltine who really kick-started regeneration after the Toxteth Riots, with the Liverpool Garden Festival. Up to 2009 FC had developed about 3,500 hectares of peri-urban woods: not much by the standards of area-obsessed foresters but what value does that land have for the people who live around it? At least 10 times that of even a popular well-managed rural forest, I'd suggest.

For me, what FC did in the urban fringe during the 2000s is an achievement on a scale comparable to the original drive for re-forestation. We are an urban, internationalist trading nation. Quality of life is crucial not just at a personal level but also to our future society and economy. I really felt for the people who have had to live next to some of the sites FC worked on, and it is hard to imagine a greater turn around than from black to green; from roaring machines, smells and dust to swathes of wildflowers.

The other lesson from the programme is that all the money, perhaps £100m in the end, was effectively competitive money: FC won the work from a range of government sources, in the same way that much of the rural conservation and recreation spend came from competitive European funding. Potential competitors were there: the Woodland Trust was in all these areas before FC, for example. The Office of the Deputy Prime Minister (ODPM) had lots of bidders but there were two problems. First, people wanted the money, but for what they wanted to do, not what the Government wanted. Second, ODPM people were very urban indeed: they knew they wanted a better environment but they had little idea what that looked like. The two organisations who were most able to present them with a vision that matched their aspirations were RSPB along the coast and FC on dry land.

Forest Vision

So what did happen at Sutton Manor? Well, there are new (plastic) windows in the houses opposite and the trees are way above head height, already a wood. The memory of the colliery is carefully preserved in the restored colliery gates and some superb sculptures. There is a new, private, housing estate filling a gap just opposite the colliery gates, and there have been murmurs that the restoration has caused affordability problems to the less well-off because house values have gone up so much. A case of 'too successful'?

But the crowning glory towers above Sutton Manor and the M62 nearby, right on the spot where Tom, Richard, Chris and I had met way back in the late '90s. *Dream* is a stunning 60ft-high sculpture of a young girl, eyes closed, dreaming, in polished concrete that shines like marble. A huge attraction, the car park was full the day I visited as people climbed the hill to stand at the foot of this stunning monument. I gather there has been the usual carping about wasting money that could have gone for jobs. The brand-new business park nearby is advertising itself as 'closest to *Dream*'. I reckon *Dream* and Sutton Manor's beautiful new woodlands will do more for jobs, for the area and for the people than any number of RDA-sponsored steel workshops – business and jobs will follow, for free, as the area and its people regain their confidence. And, of course, Martin Reynolds and the NWRDA understood that when they made the investment.

By the 2000s FC had clearly gained the confidence to get involved with some of the big emerging issues for the environment and society in England. The development of multi-purpose management, and the organisation and skills to go with it, meant FC could look broader than many others in the field. Despite its growing reputation, the future still looked uncertain; a powerful driver to new thinking. FC increasingly encountered a growing issue: the unwillingness, or simple lack of skill and understanding of many of its partner bodies to look beyond their narrow, sectoral activities.

Countryside access developed from the 'nice but non-essential of the 1960s' to a central debate on health and activity in an

Chapter 10: The Cutting Edge

increasingly overweight population. Activity, or the lack of it, has become a multi-billion pound strain on health services. FC had built a portfolio of active visitor attractions – family cycling, mountain-biking, play trails and Go Ape high wires alongside walking and special interests such as art or wildlife. A Sports Council England initiative resulted in the first purpose-designed 'Activity Centres' at Haldon near Exeter and Bedgebury in Kent. They set out to be the countryside equivalent of urban sports centres. It was a big jump for Sport England: in the South West an enlightened regional officer was fully signed up, but in the South East it took an intervention from Lord Clark and Minister Richard Caborn to swing it. Like in so many areas there remains an almost unbridgeable divide between cultures and organisations – working as we did across government departments defies gravity, and it is hard to stay on the wire for long. The statistics showed very clearly that fun activities, such as cycling and children's play, stick better than the urban gym. Helping people get active was the central and clear objective of what we were now doing, and a beautiful environment and fun activities were the method. Both sites have been very successful. The demand is huge and similar activity centres could and should be rolled out round our big cities wherever FC land allows, and hopefully to other owners' sites, including re-vitalising faded country parks.

But how to finance? FC benefitted from government capital – money that would have been spent somewhere anyway, but its increasingly business-like approach means sites like this will support their own running costs. One of the great misapprehensions about FC is the balance between public and private sector activity. Over the last 30 years FC has moved from doing almost all its work with its own labour and machinery to the opposite: during the sales debate it was suggested that 80% of business on the FC estate is now carried out by the private sector. FC is effectively the manager but not the operator; an extraordinary example of 'soft' but effective privatisation. FC, however, maintains the crucial role of striking the balance between commerce, forest users and the environment.

A Private Finance Initiative was tried to lease the opportunity to build and run visitor centres. It was a revelation after the propaganda to which public sector managers have been subjected since 1979. The medium to large companies bidding for the opportunity just did not get it. They were unimaginative – nothing new to learn for FC– risk averse and greedy. We'd hoped for new concepts that developed commercial opportunities but got bids that ranged from outlet shopping to a traditional visitor centre, where it was us, the public sector, quizzing them on where they were going to make money.

Smaller and more focussed businesses have proved very different: Go Ape is the shining example. FC invested nothing but management time and the imagination to see the opportunity, and some rent-free years till the business got going. Go Ape is original and hit a real need in modern life – to test yourself physically: to feel fear and the adrenalin rush and challenge of a 60ft drop, a 100-metre death slide. This is the private sector at its best – originality, imagination and quality – generating real, well-deserved profits, providing lots of jobs and making urban money stick in fragile rural economies. In a *Guardian* 'Guide to Extreme Sports', Go Ape got the best ratio between thrill (very exciting) and risk (very safe) of any activity.

Cycle businesses have been equally successful, with forest-based centres evolving from hire in the early days to sales, spares and repairs as demand grew. These businesses, along with the best catering franchises, are characterised by people with expertise and commitment – they like doing what they are doing, they like working with their customers, they are not just there to shave the largest possible profits. That has been a problem with some larger catering firms which often seem to belong to the 'get away with it' economy: the opposite and worst end of the private sector, dependent on a depressing balancing act along the margins of what is acceptable – high prices, high profits, minimum resource and marginal customer satisfaction – sadly what you all too often get from crude, dogmatic

Chapter 10: The Cutting Edge

privatisation. In contrast, imaginative partnership between private and public can have huge benefits: jobs in the Dalby Valley have rocketed from a low of 15 after forestry mechanised in the 1980s to over 50 today, whilst Westonbirt Arboretum more than doubled its employment at the same time reducing a 50% cash deficit to break even. Real value for the taxpayer.

In the urban fringe, we had always been aware of the potential for sites to coalesce as more were developed, but a bigger potential is starting to emerge. FC thinking matched architect Sir Terry Farrell's concept of 'parklands' in the Thames Gateway: not a green grid but a substantial, contiguous area of land for people and wildlife. Patterns are already building: when FC bought Jeskyns Farm it found Woodland Trust woodland as its direct neighbour, their wood adjoined Shorne Country Park to the north, a Repton landscape in restoration to the east and beyond it Ranscombe Farm, a Plantlife Nature Reserve. RSPB had Cliffe Marshes to the north-east and subsequently took over the management of the foreshore towards Gravesend, only a few fields from the country park. North of the Thames, Rainham Marshes stands at the shorewood end of the Ingrebourne river. FC acquired what is now Ingrebourne Hill, which adjoins the earlier Hornchurch Country Park to the north, there is a gap of one farm and then Pages Wood – new woodland on what were arable fields.

With so much happening in just a decade what could the future look like? From a management perspective it is time to think about how different land links up, trails designed to join together, not just loops in each individual piece of land. It affects how each new area is designed: at a site in the northwest we looked at retreating a sea wall – if it were just the single site it would go back one step, but the prospects for the whole peninsula – dominated by a landfill site and existing nature reserve – suggested a much larger sweep; taking it back two steps, two-thirds of the whole site.

We started probing wider benefits; in particular water management, and Marion Spain of the Environment Agency who 'got' the whole idea introduced 'blue-green' or 'turquoise' infrastructure: land working for water management alongside people and wildlife. We started thinking about just how much benefit – making less intensively managed land work harder and harder for people and the environment – it might be possible to generate. Far from each site having to be the same – identical facilities, identical access and objectives, for example – it became clear that the sort of hidden zoning FC had practised for years would work well in an area like Gravesend – Jeskyns and Shorne Country Park taking the brunt of general visitor use; trails, signing and car parking giving a degree of protection to the nature reserves.

However, getting others to think the same way is not easy: I was disappointed that RSPB, who have done such a good job along the foreshore, did not bite despite my probing. The same problem that ODPM encountered seems deeply embedded: our approach to land use is totally siloed and the conservation bodies do conservation, access bodies do recreation and so on. It was a similar story with 'Green Arc', which we set up with key supporters at Epping Forest who had very definitely got the message, and others in the northeast axis around London. The problem here, very relevant to the localism debate, was that as local authority engagement increased the scale of ambition died away.

There also remains the strong perception that agriculture must always be the most important land use – even some Forestry Commissioners questioned the development of Jeskyns, on the doorstep of 50,000 people, because it was Grade 1 agricultural land. Back in the 1960s agricultural land on the edge of cities was seen as needing protection from people. Because there has never been any real review of how we use land, that perception persists, strongly, despite the fact that when urban interests decide to move they will always trump any other land use – generally without even being aware of what they are doing.

The foundations are there for a complete change in how we 'finish' our towns and cities – access, wilderness and wildlife on

Chapter 10: The Cutting Edge

people's doorsteps, a real impact on how our children grow up, how active we are with all the spin-off impacts on obesity and social cohesion. The groundwork has been done but can the different organisations up their game, come out of their silos and join across the social-environment divide to create something worthy of the 21st century?

The New Forest in particular pulled together a wide range of interests in a major landuse programme. Supported by the depth of background FC has in multi-purpose planning, we decided to move on in a considered way from the individual conservation or access projects to an approach that pulled them together into a single entity. The Neroche Forest on the northern slopes of the Blackdowns had been a problem area for decades. Steep wet soils with small bogs and landslips had defeated FC's efforts to coniferise the native woodland: conifers actually grew beautifully, producing some fine stands but despite the prodigious efforts of earlier foresters they survived in isolated pockets amongst a jumble of broad-leafed woodland mixed with failing conifer. Rare unimproved grassland was a haven for butterflies – but isolated by the woodland and declining fast due to lack of scale.

We set out to transform this forest and with the ambition to hit all three legs of sustainability – social, environmental and economic – at the heart of the project: returning the forest to native broadleaves and open habitat – including developing huge pasture woodland corridors – for the environment, developing access by linking and improving trails for the social side and, through an increase in visitors, developing business opportunities in a fragile economy.

Rather than just being a conservation project this was thinking about the future of rural areas in the round. The project won a Heritage Lottery Fund (HLF) 'Landscape Partnership' grant. The next innovation was the genuine lead given to local people through a New Forest style forum approach. Along with a range of imaginative projects, including grazing organic Longhorn Cattle in the new pasture woodland, local engagement clarified the need to make existing jobs more secure over creating a lot of new jobs.

But, again, it has proved very difficult to communicate this sort of thinking. In the case of Neroche, halfway through developing the project plan the managers had to break it back into its individual elements because they simply could not get the message of the whole across: so they talked to conservationists about conservation, to walkers and horse riders about access and so on. FC has continued with a new HLF programme, long in the making, in Wyre Forest and I am involved with another Somerset project, the Avalon Marshes, modelled on similar lines – a local partnership initially led by imaginative Natural England staff who got the message and are now increasingly handing over to the local community.

I had been most concerned to focus on the lowlands because, traditionally, it has been too easy simply to push land use issues to the uplands – still referred to, by many, as the 'nation's green lungs'. The uplands are great, but not when the main motivation for doing new things there is to remove them from the agricultural lobby's heartlands. However, the Wild Ennerdale project, which drew in the National Trust and United Utilities, has been very successful. The coniferisation of Ennerdale was notorious and design improvements to its upper margins were central case studies on FC landscape-training courses in the 1970s. It was not till I visited, however, that I saw the stunning rockscapes that never featured in the landscape re-designs. Some were swamped by tree planting, others made invisible from the valley. Steep slopes made replanting expensive and a new approach was clearly needed. Rather than going on down the less, better-designed conifer route a new idea of an extensive wilderness area developed. Now, with extensive grazing as the main management tool broadleaves and open space are developing and water quality improving in what is becoming a landscape with an increasingly wild and natural feel to it. It has been great to have the National Trust as a partner – but disappointing that nearly 10 years on this is still their exemplar project: with their

Chapter 10: The Cutting Edge

huge estate, and I would include the near-invisible land held as investment rather than for its heritage value, the potential for exciting ideas without the need to buy new land could be incredible, not least closer to where people live.

We faced the same sort of problem in Suffolk where the 'Eastern Horizon' idea looked for a wider vision for habitat restoration than the RSPB's heathland-focussed campaign. It was a campaign redolent of the 1980s, and particularly problematic within forestry because of the direct challenge to tree growing, and with it FC's basic remit – the forester's response was 'we're the Forestry, not the heathland, Commission'. In the New Forest the holistic approach to land management had absorbed both foresters' and public concerns about heathland. The RSPB campaign, which took the form of a very critical, single-minded attack focussed solely on heathland pointed up the issue as sharply as it could. I found it particularly difficult because, as we have so little semi-natural habitat left, I support saving what we can – but in the absence of any sort of wider forestry policy the RSPB position is vulnerable: they had largely ignored de-forestation and carbon issues and failed to make any connection with losing forest in one place against gains in others. It was a problem that could have been solved if they had understood the opportunities they were already opening up on the urban fringe. So much of what has worked has been about making imaginative linkages: current thinking is so silo driven that big opportunities are being missed. Would the forestry sales fiasco have happened had RSPB used its power to force a new remit for FC before the 2010 elections?

What was hidden behind this whole debate was FC's vital role in delivering large-scale habitat restoration. Removing trees has not been popular with local people. RSPB had an excoriating time restoring heathland, prosecuted for illegal felling in Dorset following public protests, learning the lessons but still finding it hard going on later projects at Farnham Heath and Sandy. The FC, facing the same problems and working very hard on them, has restored roughly 10 times RSPB's restoration and may well have restored as much as all the other conservation organisations put together: that FC has more restorable heath than anyone else was the public part of the campaign, but that restoration depended on FC's delivery skills was never stated.

The FC has shown the way to a very different world, a world where real imagination and a willingness to break down self-imposed barriers could find the space in our small, heavily populated country for so much more of what different interests want. RSPB want more heathland. Carbon & deforestation are serious vulnerabilities. The Woodland Trust wants more woodland. The private sector forestry and industry organisation Confor is concerned about the loss of conifer timber, so why not some mixed woods? With cross-sectoral support they could be much bigger, especially if they breathed life into the carbon code. Could multi-purpose versus industrial plantations be a bigger woodland issue than species now? The Woodland Trust wants its woods closer to people: The Ramblers could build a new access agenda based on the rapidly extending peri-urban network of wilder land, led by FC, RSPB & Woodland Trust (WT) delivery. And perhaps an early example could set a planning precedent by attaching a large area of wilder woodland/habitat/open access to a housing development? The National Trust?

Renewable energy and the low carbon economy is on the brink of radically changing forestry and wood production. It has been a slow start: government policy has been heavily focussed on electricity and either the very largest or very smallest scales from Drax to solar panels on the roof. In a field driven by industry lobbies and adventurous technology, tiny, poorly represented and outdated wood didn't get a look in. Eventually, however, the government made the link between biomass and heat and commissioned former NFU President Sir Ben Gill to produce a report. Gill pointed out that 49% of all our energy use is heat. It can, of course, be supplied by electricity but by far the greater part is gas or oil. Bluntly, we can

Chapter 10: The Cutting Edge

switch off our computers and put cooking oil in our cars until we're blue in the face – but if we do not tackle heat we might as well not bother. As the report approached its conclusion I attended a high-level meeting at Defra and, very late in the day and rather tentatively, put my hand up and suggested wood might have a role to play. Rebecca Cowburn, secretary to Ben Gill's group, picked it, and following a flurry of activity wood got into the report and FC was commissioned to produce a woodfuel strategy.

The wood is already out there: at least one million tonnes from unmanaged woodland and another one million from clean waste wood (we import 80% of our wood needs), equivalent to heating 250,000 homes, not earth shattering but about equivalent in energy saving to cutting the speed limit to 50mph. Which looks the more politically saleable? It also became clear that the wood, mostly available in quite small units, matched well with rural areas without access to mains gas. The strategy is aimed firmly at relatively local, small-scale rather than large-scale, centralised, use, with woodchip as the main fuel for boilers from maybe 30 Kw to 500 Kw – heating for a large house to a large office. The approach followed experience – brought into FC by Andy Hall in particular – from other countries, especially Austria where modern wood-burning systems provide much of the heat in rural areas.

Worcestershire County Council's offices were a good early example at the upper end of the scale. Ideal is the estate with a stately home supplied from its own woods using existing equipment and spare labour at slack times. These ideas were against the general drift of renewable policy, with big companies scouting for wood volume and advocating planting of fast-growing agricultural or tree crops. They had failed largely through being too mean, not even guaranteeing farmer growers that they would take what they grew, let alone at a set price. I went against this route because timber from small woods is unlikely to be 'industrially mobile', much better sourced at a local scale for local use. I didn't think traffic planners in the South East of England would have welcomed the 15,000 new

40-tonne lorry movements needed to concentrate the region's wood volume to a few big centres! The big users clearly expected starvation prices and were ready to switch sources at the whim of world markets. Once a boiler is installed in a local school it is going to need wood for its 20-year life. Local woods and local suppliers ensure energy security.

Renewable energy should complement the environment movement. Sadly, that is all too often not the case: industries such as wind and tidal power have not given sufficient thought to wider environmental impacts until after the protests have started. In contrast, the biggest issue for England's woods is lack of management, and the declining biodiversity that results. Bringing more woods back into management and operating at the small, local, scale of many of those woods, wood energy is one of those rare win-wins.

It is interesting to reflect on where a conventional government consultation might have led. All views are taken into account and amalgamated into a whole by skilled people, but with no particular insight into the issue: we listened and learned but came up with a proposal that incorporated experience and judgement into a genuinely original and innovative approach. It cut firmly across the more obvious big industrial approach.

Once again, we were working across departmental boundaries, with Defra working with the Business Department (responsibilities later transferred to the new Department for Energy and Climate Change, DECC). Rebeca Cowburn worked tirelessly across the government system to promote what has turned out to be one of the most successful outcomes of Ben Gill's project. Within FC Emma Harding did most of the hard work on the report, whilst Ian Tubby was setting up the Biomass Energy Centre advice service within Forest Research. The support we got once people had grasped the concept was gratifying; The Country Land and Business Association (CLA) is not noted for being government-friendly, so Chief Surveyor Oliver Harwood's vigorous support throughout was a slightly unexpected bonus – he'd got it and realised just what

Chapter 10: The Cutting Edge

it could do for his woodland-owning members. I loved the comment from one landowner as he commissioned his new boiler 'I'm warm for the first time in my life'!

The delivery plan I proposed was a conventional grant and skills-based government intervention approach. What actually emerged, brokered by Angela Duignan who took over the policy from me, was the Renewable Heat Incentive (RHI) – a government subsidy for each Kilowatt produced, paid to the owner of small- to medium-sized boilers. It applies to all biomass and other heat sources like ground pump heat. Solar is far more expensive: it takes a subsidy more than double for wood to make it viable – God's solar panel, the tree, is still well ahead of man's invention.

Heat from wood is building fast but from a low base of around 2,000 installations. Wood supply and price varies hugely, from clean waste wood where suppliers are just pleased not to have to pay landfill charges right up to bagged firewood and kindling on garage forecourts which can return astronomic prices. The way things are developing there will be locally based businesses supplying locally. Scale is increasing: big chippers are taking over from hand-fed roadside chippers. The biggest travel around, munching through piles of stacked wood at as much as 200 tonnes/hour. As predicted, redundant stock yards and barns work well as chip storage and drying areas. Although pellets are easier to handle and feed to automatic boilers, their much-higher cost may well lead to chips winning out – it is a bit of a VHS vs Betamax situation at present. Installation quality remains a recurring problem: poor design, over specification, pricing that reflects the lack of knowledge of most buyers. The common problems include:

• Overspecified boilers – wood boilers run best flat out, so plan for 90% of maximum demand, not 120%. A big header tank is the answer – run the boiler hard, store the hot water in a big tank and use the heat while the boiler rests. And, if it is fitted, keep your existing system – it may be easier and more economic to run oil or gas in the 'shoulder' months when you only need a little heat.

Forest Vision

- Badly designed wood/chip handling – often through lack of space. And, as a result, long augurs which carry the chips from store to boiler – the augur is the weak link, always vulnerable to jamming. Keep it short.
- Fuel quality – moisture is important – but it is chip quality that is the key – chips from ordinary 'reduction' chippers, the sort most tree surgeons use, will contain outsize chips guaranteed to jam the augur. Precision chips fall within a much-narrower range and feed better.
- Long pipe runs between buildings: the best prospects are buildings with a 'wet' central heating system already installed – whip out the coal or oil boiler and pop in wood and away you go. Fitting wet systems, and especially joining scattered, buildings can get massively costly – several times the basic boiler costs.

And some boilers work better than others – the Austrians have been practising for a long time, a lot of their rural areas run on wood and run well.

Wood is much better used for heat than electricity generation. Electricity generation on its own is only 25% efficient in using the energy, a wood boiler 90%. One way round is combined heat and power. You need somewhere to use the heat; so, not much good for a remote Scottish village, and the combined plant is more costly and complicated.

And as your toes warm up, remember you're saving bluebells, nightingales and dormice at the same time. Not many heat sources you can say that for!

I am holding my breath in the hope this stunning new industry gets off the ground and fast. The evidence is it will: RHI is right. But I am also holding it because there is one fly in the ointment: the risk that as prices rise wood will simply switch from existing industries that use wood too small for sawn timber. These include the paper and panel board businesses making products that include chipboard, orientated strandboard (OSB or Stirlingboard), medium-density fibreboard (MDF) and the carton board milk containers are

Chapter 10: The Cutting Edge

made from. It would be a serious failure were a new, subsidised industry to outcompete existing businesses solely through government money. That is bad. It gets worse. Wood that switches saves not one gram of carbon, in fact it probably wastes it because panel board, like sawn timber, 'locks up' carbon for longer. Yes, the trees recapture carbon from burning, but wood going into construction could be there for 20, 50, 100 years. This is why the UK Forest Products Association (UKFPA) reacted so strongly against the sales of the most 'commercial' woods like Kielder, as did the conservative MP for Hexham: Egger's, a foreign investor, has just spent £100m renewing the chipboard mill at the heart of his constituency – and its wood comes from Kielder, just up the road. Confor has called for a 'level playing field' for carbon, and they are right. I do not know how you do it, but the unique value of wood, perhaps our most sustainable material, needs to be recognised across the board. We'll get there, but UKFPA is right to see FC as vital to ensuring continuity of supply as government moves to even competition between equally valuable uses of wood.

This is where the future starts.

There are two obvious, big, directions for FC and forestry in England:

• The first is around our towns and cities. FC has reached a point where it has demonstrated just what trees and forests can do for 'liveability'. It is putting the missing positive into our damaged green belts. If we can let our imaginations fly, where are the limits? Just how close can we bring the countryside to more and more people? Could England become unique in the world in the way it surrounds with beauty the places we all live?

• The second – and this brings in the whole of our forests and woodlands and their owners and managers – is the low carbon economy and climate change. Forests are not going to solve the problem, but what they can contribute really matters: as we use energy more efficiently, bring neglected woods into management and plant more trees, its contribution will rise and rise. A 50% gain in energy efficiency, for example, will raise the homes warmed by biomass from 250,000 to 500,000. The Woodfuel Strategy only assumes half of the neglected woodland being brought into management, and 250,000 ha of new woodland could easily be created by 2050.

In the background to all this, but politically critical at the moment, is the state vs private-sector debate. Yes, selling all the woods and cutting FC staff and costs are one way. There is another; the route FC has pursued quite consciously over the last decade: expanding the state away. FC actually took on more staff as it did more work, but for every new recruit it probably generated 3-4 private-sector jobs. More work means greater productivity – FC's central services did not expand even when it won 25% of its income as extra, external funding. That is real efficiency: cutting costs, people and services is not. Efficiency is about doing more for the same or less, not just cutting. FC's dominance in timber has been a big issue. There is a simple answer: when prices rise woods must be brought back into management. The traditional private sector is sitting on unexploited conifer and could double output from the current 500,000 tonnes to the one million achieved in the past. Then there is the one million tonnes from neglected woodland and, hey presto, as FC's output remains steady, as a proportion of England's total timber production it would drop from 60% to just 30%.

But where will government find their lost millions? It is simple: wood for energy, the Woodfuel Strategy, could generate as much as £600m per annum of new business. The investment in the boilers to use the wood could be as high as £1 billion. This is growth: it is jobs, it is there for the long term; not a single capital hit that quickly turns into a minus as new owners come begging for grants. This is double-value money because so much will flow to intractable, impoverished rural areas.

Chapter 11

Privatisation 2: 2010-11

That a new Conservative Government would take an interest in forestry was predictable. What was surprising was the unexpected scale of the Government's ambitions, matched only by its disorganisation. Accelerated disposals were no surprise, given the state of national finances. The first indication of what was planned was Jim Paice's announcement of 15%, 40,000 hectares, of sales to raise £100 million over five years. That might have been possible, and taking the slice of least public benefit woods improved the prospects for sale and cash value. The proposed speed and scale would have stretched the market, potentially reducing values, and the area would almost certainly have overlapped woods people valued and would fight to save.

However, shortly afterwards the intention to sell the whole estate – largely on ideological rather than cash grounds – was announced, and things started getting complicated. The speed with which public opposition grew, finding a route through the 38 Degrees web petition, shocked even foresters who had been through it all before. That *The Telegraph* group criticised not just the sale but the way it was being carried out from an early stage should have raised alarm bells in government. Key was the very obvious fact, even without insider knowledge, that the FC was being kept well out of the whole process – it was easy to spot which bits had FC input and which bits did not. Government proposals were littered with glaring inaccuracies, reflecting the level of forestry knowledge in Defra in the absence of FC support. It was uncanny how closely events mirrored 1993-4: on 4th January 2011, as the issue really started to hot up, I wrote to Caroline Spelman saying that 'you will find the sale value of the forests will go down at roughly the same rate as the political cost goes up'. I had not actually anticipated that as the cash value fell to zero the politics would eventually cost the Secretary of State her job.

When, eventually, the consultation document emerged, it was already so complex as to be undeliverable, even with the full weight of FC expertise behind it. It had already hit a host of bumps, even ignoring public pressure. It was suggested that 15% was the limit government could sell without primary legislation. That never came up in 1993-94. This time it meant clauses in the unpopular Public Services bill, to permit the sale of the whole estate, without further reference to Parliament, and presented in the Lords before the consultation was announced. It was already subject to vigorous debate, it made for an uncomfortable birth for the consultation into an already unfriendly world. It was recognised that some forests could not be sold on the open market – particularly the Dean and New Forest – and then a rump of about 10% emerged of leasehold and other forests with legal constraints meaning they were likely to be hard to sell. In pursuit of the 'Big Society' the Government had decided charities should take what was defined as 'Heritage Forests', those perceived to have the highest social and environmental value, and had given an inside track to the Woodland Trust and the National Trust. The Woodland Trust now insisted woods with Plantations on Ancient Woodland Sites should not be sold until restored, so out came another chunk of early sales, including some small woods which were of otherwise low value, so new woods had to be found to sell to replace them. Events did not progress far enough for it to emerge that the largely coniferous substitutes overlapped heavily with RSPB ambitions for heathland restoration.

Throughout Jim Paice failed to recognise the difference between legally protected access under the Countryside and Rights Of Way Act (CRoW) and the 'higher rights' – cycling, riding and

Chapter 11: Privatisation 2: 2010-11

other sports and activities; nor could the Government accept that whilst the law might enforce access the welcome might be very different. There was an entertaining twist when, searching the jumble cupboard for props, Caroline Spelman came up with the old chestnut of the FC conflict as simultaneous land-managing poacher and regulatory gamekeeper. The trouble was Jim Paice had told a Lords Committee that, because of the quality of UK Woodland Assurance Scheme certification, he saw no need for woods to be both certified and regulated by FC – a neat bit of de-regulation which I personally support. In doing so he had just completely scotched the case for a real conflict were the fully certified FC estate to fall outside FC regulation altogether: which is why the conflict was hurriedly converted into the even less convincing old chestnut of FC unfairly dominating the timber market – a domination which the UK Forest Products Association was very vociferously arguing FOR.

Just two documents had FC written all over them: the map classifying the estate and the Impact Assessment – a more detailed paper in particular laying out the financials. It had Jim Paice's signature on the front and it said the Government would not make any money out of selling the Estate because the proceeds would soon be returned to the new owners through the Government grants the land would now be entitled to, and it was almost certainly right – I only found one error in the whole document, whilst most other parts of the exercise were riddled with simple mistakes.

As events got hotter and hotter it also became clear that the major NGOs – especially NT & WT which increasingly appeared to be in cahoots with the Government – were not on the same wavelength as the public: almost all the NGOs had reacted by accepting this was going to happen and started debating the conditions they would like to see imposed. The public reaction was a simple and resounding 'no', a 'no' that reverberated through a 550,000 signature petition and exceptional postbags to MPs in FC woodland constituencies. Just as this issue had shocked the Government, equally it was unprecedented for NGOs who for a decade had assumed the right to speak for their members on political issues. The Government got the message. They had little option. Whether the NGOs did remains to be seen: on the day the Government backed down, Fiona Reynolds of the National Trust appeared to agree with Matthew D'Ancona on the Today programme that the Prime Minister was right – that it was a 'presentational issue' which would have been fine presented properly. If you believe that you will believe anything.

The Prime Minister also contributed the thought, just days before the whole thing collapsed, that the National Trust and Woodland Trust would do a much better job of managing than the FC. Whilst the forestry profession was, understandably, split on the rights and wrongs of selling FC land, it was united in the view that there was no way these charities were competent to take over from FC – not least because neither is managing their woodland holdings particularly effectively at the moment. It took an excoriating blast from Jonathon Porritt, roundly condemning their stance and the sheer effrontery of suggesting they were capable of taking on the task, before they reluctantly backed down and announced that they did not think they could do the job.

The Commons debate leading up to the withdrawal of the proposals was extraordinary. Mary McCreagh for the Opposition was much better briefed than Caroline Spelman because she had been briefed, as she was legally entitled to be, by the forestry trades unions. Caroline Spelman had not had the same benefit because ministers had cut FC out of the loop. I felt, and still do, rather sorry for Caroline Spelman. How on earth did she get so deeply embroiled in something that clearly came from Jim Paice who should have been left to struggle with his massive mistake on his own?

When Mrs Spelman went to the international Nagoya conference the same year she talked a lot of sense about some really important issues and, whilst it may have won her no friends, she said things that needed saying about agricultural subsidies. Impressive, in an age when politicians are derided, was the quality of the backbench

Chapter 11: Privatisation 2: 2010-11

speeches from all sides of the house. These were forest constituency MPs who clearly had put a lot of work into accurate and penetrating speeches about what the National Forests are really about. Only the television picture distinguished which side members were on as opprobrium was heaped on the Government with little regard to party loyalties.

The Commons debate did not go well for the Government, however you look at it. Just a few days later the Prime Minister floored the Leader of the Opposition when to the question 'are you happy with your forestry policy?' the PM replied 'No'. Ed Milliband was silenced: no one had prepared for this.

Next day it all collapsed, the consultation was withdrawn and an 'expert panel', a classic late-night Civil Service face-saver, was announced. Though with obvious weaknesses, the panel's constitution was a good deal more thoughtful than what had gone before. It is hard to see how the Government's approach could have been anything other than a mess. The killer was mixed objectives: it had to be either a money raiser or political dogma; it was never, ever going to work both together, however insightful the preparation and presentation might have been.

There has been speculation about the FC role, with Government apparently blaming it for the collapse of the process. It is to blame in a number of ways. Perhaps, most of all, it is what this book is about – 20 years of concerted effort to exit from the stink of the Flow Country, to get close to the people who love the forests and give them what they want. That is not a crime. Not appreciating that this is what had happened is, however, foolish. It is particularly so when FC has lived out localism within the body of a traditional central government department – easy to miss, especially if you don't ask.

FC is also to blame for not giving a warning – but then it appears it was not allowed to and would have been seen as obstructive had it done so. And, in truth, there are not that many people who went through 1993-94 left today, absolutely no one in Defra which didn't even exist and clearly the Conservative party has (probably wisely) dispensed with its race memory from the mid 1990s. Finally, the suspicion will be that FC briefed against the Government. I do not believe that is so – as a serving Civil Servant I would not have done, nor did I in 1993-4. People like me know the facts which FC would have given ministers had they asked – my letter of 4th January 2011 to Mrs Spelman, no doubt long since shredded and recycled, spelt out my view from my experience. The only thing I got wrong was just how high the issue blew and how quickly it collapsed. I have been careful throughout this process not even to distort what I have said in public, let alone lie. I told Mrs Spelman that, whilst fundamentally against forest sales, I accept from experience that there are FC woods delivering limited public benefit which could be sold with little or no impact. Similarly, I support Jim Paice's suggestion that UKWAS certification does not require FC regulation. I suspect my former colleagues will have been glad not to have been asked. As a Civil Servant I would have felt morally obliged to give the best possible advice and, being fairly ingenious, might well have found some ways through that others would have missed. There is little doubt that an FC supported by government to raise money might well have sold at least half the 40,000 hectares and very probably made a good deal more than half the £100m target.

So what was behind the protest? It is not really for me to say. Most foresters, FC and private sector, care passionately about forestry, and in particular take sustainability, replacing the trees they remove, as an unquestionable given. Some of the finest timber forests are also the most stunningly beautiful. However, foresters tend to be relatively calm and rational. Even for people who have devoted a lifetime to the National Forests the public response to the sales proposals was stunning and, to be honest, quite humbling. There is no way I would try to grab too much credit for FC as opposed to the forests themselves, but I think FC had a part to play. I do not think there would have been this support for a body as reviled as forestry has been in the not too distant past and the reaction

Chapter 11: Privatisation 2: 2010-11

of the people FC worked most closely with in forests like the Dean can only be pleasing. FC still talks about 'recreation', implying a bit of fun on the side of life. I don't think that comes anywhere near describing people's feelings for the forests. I realised years ago just how important forests can be in people's lives – people who walk their dogs twice a day; perhaps people whose friends and lifestyle outside work may be defined by mountain biking or walking in the forests.

I have sensed a bit more, however, and that is the extent to which both the dream and reality of the forests actually goes quite deep into our national identity – there has always been this idealised view of the English countryside, the green and pleasant land generations of citizen soldiers went abroad to fight for. A countryside, as has frequently been pointed out, owned by someone else, not the urban majority. I wonder whether the FC's nationally owned forests really have achieved supremely the perception of genuine national ownership – something we really do all share. I hope so. It is certainly what my FC colleagues and I have worked for.

That is the easy bit. The 'invisible man' in all this has been the supporters of the sale. The Government's proposal has all the atmosphere of a rural-landowning dinner party – the rather vague grumblings round the table, blaming Defra and of course the EU. But the grumbling audience are well removed from the real forests and today's FC. Perhaps they are from Jim Paice's southern Suffolk constituency, not well known for its woodland and FC ownership? The Country Landowners Association were probably in there, but with rather limited aims, perhaps grabbing back resented leaseholds bought by FC in the hard times of the 1930s, or perhaps a neighbouring block of woodland that would add to an estate.

The people who sell forests, and forestry investment companies, were amongst the most vociferous supporters – they would be, wouldn't they? A wider group of private foresters will have seen opportunities – although few, I suspect, would have gone for the triple 'whammy' in preference to an accelerated sales programme including some larger blocks. Their view would have focussed on timber – and, perhaps more importantly, capital land values – with limited understanding of the wider values, and an expectation that Government would protect buyers from the wrath of the public. Bigger forestry companies, more active in Wales and Scotland might well have bought the whole picture and taken on FC's commercially successful recreation enterprises alongside the timber.

But that is history. What happens next?

Chapter 12

Future Forests

The future began in February 2011 when Prime Minister David Cameron replied 'No' to Opposition leader Ed Milliband's question 'Is the Prime Minister happy with his forestry policy?'

In a classic civil service overnight solution, when Secretary of State Caroline Spelman went to the House to apologise the following day, she announced the establishment of an Independent Forestry Panel (IFP) under the Chairmanship of James Jones, Bishop of Liverpool, who was to become even better known for his Chairmanship of the enquiry into the Hillsborough disaster. But it has been slow progress since then, with many a twist and turn.

Although the Panel published its report in just over a year, nearly three years on, in February 2014, the future of the Forestry Commission forests is still not resolved. In the meantime, both Caroline Spelman and Jim Paice lost their ministerial jobs at the first reshuffle, replaced by Owen Paterson and David Heath, the latter departing himself only a year later to be replaced by Dan Rogerson.

I joined a ginger group – 'Our Forests', led by Jonathon Porritt – to watch and comment on developing policy, and also worked for the Institute of Chartered Foresters, first on their response to the (aborted) consultations on the sale of the forests and later on their input to the IFP. I talked to a lot of people and followed a wide range of media. Some people 'got it', the big picture of forestry and the FC described so far. Others, often knowledgeable in one area, simply did not. 'What is the State doing growing trees?' pretty well sums it up and, of course, they are right; were FC no more than a timber business the State would have no place. Nature conservationists

Forest Vision

tended to have a similar view – not doing enough for heathland or for ancient woods. This theme of whether people have 'got it' or not has run through the whole three-year story since February 2011 and, as I'll explain, holds the secret to the Future Forests.

So, what are the key issues?

The first is what most of this book is overtly about: it is the combining and balancing of a range of different benefits on a single area of land. It directly opposes the simple, single-product approach that dominates current landuse thinking. It crosses sectors, bringing together everything from beauty to hard products such as timber, often in the same places at the same time.

The skill the FC has brought to this multi-purpose, multi-benefit management is the skill to manage different interests, to separate by gentle guidance the walkers and the cyclists, to steer people and forest operations around nature conservation interests, to plan so that profitable operations complement, not conflict with, environmental priorities.

The second is more difficult and probably even more important: it is the feel people have for the countryside and the landscape and, in particular, 'their' bit of that landscape. It may be where they walk their dog or ride their horse every day from a home nearby, it may be where they mountain-bike or walk at the weekend, or where they go on holiday. This love of the countryside goes beyond simply 'use': surely it is a key part of that most elusive thing, the English national identity?

Forestry Commission forests seem to have evolved from the rather forbidding face of a government department to something people really do genuinely feel they own and feel are hugely important to them. It is an emotional connection as much as a rational one and it is justified. Fortunately, the attempts to reduce England's forests to no more than the neat row of perfect timber sticks of the harshest traditional forester's imagination are doomed to failure.

The forests are incredible, varied and beautiful from the sweep of a huge landscape to the turning over of a fallen oak leaf on the

Chapter 12: Future Forests

forest floor. It is impossible to make individual experience of the forests fit a supermarket shelf, and in the forests it is possible to hide from the mobile phone salesmen who claim to know more about us than we do ourselves. It is from experiences playing in dens in the forest our children will grow up to be self-sufficient, imaginative, lively and brilliant; and in my old age I want to be able to trundle to the view over the forest in my electric buggy!

That the people who love the forests and rose against the sales are hard to pin down – not well represented by established pressure groups whether for nature conservation, timber or access – makes the issue politically more difficult, but none the less vital.

What the forests mean to people is, on our crowded island, by far the most important value of the Forestry Commission's nationally owned forests. In 2010 the Economics for the Environment Consultancy (Eftec) published a report commissioned by the FC: *The economic contribution of the Public Forest Estate in England*. In the role of forestry consultant I supported the leader, Ian Dickie. Taking the complex results to a very simple level, Eftec rated the value of the benefits the public forests deliver as follows: People: 3, Carbon: 2, Timber: 1, Biodiversity: 1.

It is against this background that the IFP were selected and worked. Would the Panel 'get it'? That was a very open question when the membership was announced: there were many of the names from the conservation sector who had been ready to take over FC forests but there was not even a suggestion of representation from the people and groups that had led the opposition to the government sell-off plans.

There were also representatives from forestry and the landowning sector. Contrary to what might have been expected, although there were some noisy voices from forestry urging the sell-off, the key timber and land organisations, especially Confor and the UK Forest Products Association (UKFPA), were strongly and consistently opposed to the plans which threatened to undermine established forest industries.

Forest Vision

I worked with Our Forests to produce '*A Vision for England's woods and forests*', and a wide range of organisations and individuals gave their views to the Panel. The Panel worked very hard, visiting forests and people across the country. My fear was that they would go the way of the Foresight study on landuse and produce a sector by sector wish list. Clearly, there was intense debate and I understand it was not until the final stages that agreement developed; but it was worth it. The Panel 'got it': 'To say that our woodlands are vital is not an exaggeration' James Jones said in his Foreword, and clearly he was not the only panel member who had been on a personal journey through the Panel process.

The panel 'got' all the big issues in English forestry. At the heart of the recommendations, and what this is really all about, they put forward a range of safeguards for the estate: a new, independent, body owning the public forests in trust for the nation, with a charter setting out its aims, and a group of Guardians to ensure it follows them.

The new management body should focus on a 'triple bottom line', meaning that it should aim to balance the priorities of people, the environment and economics.

They emphasised the urgency of bringing more of England's woodlands into management: with nearly half (500,000 hectares) not in active management, wildlife is suffering and low carbon fuel and materials are going to waste.

They identified the threat posed to trees, and everything to do with woodlands and forests, by new diseases of trees, both native and imported – and this was before the *Chalara* disease of Ash was found in the UK, deepening an already serious crisis.

The Panel also pointed out that there are many woods close to where people live that are not open for access. They stressed that woods that people can use are of the highest importance: there is a big opportunity already there to open more woods to people and to plant new woods for public access. The Panel pushed for a big increase in England's forest cover, from the present 10% to 15% and,

Chapter 12: Future Forests

crucially, urged the creation of 'a new woodland culture' with the Forestry Commission's Forest Services charged with championing, protecting and increasing the benefits from trees, woodlands and forests. That, they say, is about getting people to think differently, so that woodlands and wood products are appreciated in everyday life.

The Panel gave the government – and especially the Conservative party – a route map out of the forest sales nightmare. Would the government grasp the opportunity?

Its first reaction was to agree with everything the Panel recommended – generally the sign that government intends to do no such thing, and so it proved. Hidden in the small print was the suggestion, directly contrary to the Panel recommendation, that the new organisation should be run by a Board chaired by the Secretary of State's nominee with members selected through the Public Appointments system – effectively selected by Defra civil servants.

It became worse as detail was added by the Defra paper '*Management organisation: Governance premises Summary*' issued in July 2013. It became clear that, far from anyone taking charge and doing the political sums, a classic civil service fudge was taking place, with each consultee around government getting their say:

'It will not be a Crown body and its staff will not be civil servants' – obviously coming from the Cabinet Office, trying to push everything possible out of the public sector.

'The PFE (Public Forest Estate) would have a strong focus on generating income through trading and commercial activities, including timber production' which looked like the Treasury view, or if not the Treasury itself, Defra concerned to do what they expected Treasury to demand. A statement that clearly overrides the Panel's 'triple bottom line' which aims to balance objectives.

'The PFE Chair would be appointed by Defra Ministers in line with existing practice and guidance' ... 'The Secretary of State would have a reserved power of direction' ... 'There would be a group of Guardians (as proposed by the Panel).... However, there would be

Forest Vision

no question of the Guardians being a second Board for the PFE or having responsibility for managing the organisation in any way.' This sounds like Defra unable to conceive of letting go, in direct contradiction to the Panel recommendation but also to its own proposal that the new organisation cannot be a Crown body.

Defra unable to conceive of letting go – and a position impossible to reconcile with the government's own proposal that 'it will not be a Crown Body' nor the Panel's advocacy of independence.

Governance is a dry subject – but fraught with risk. The structure proposed could easily produce another Railtrack – a Board packed by public appointment with people with no real interest or knowledge of the subject, but largely concerned with squeezing out money to hand back to the Treasury. The Railtrack story spelt out the risks all too starkly: a Board more concerned with property dealing than running the railway leading to a fatal train crash.

FC's commercial development has depended on taking people with it. Trust is crucial and there is unlikely to be trust in a government-appointed board. Even now there is a risk around 'Forest Holidays', floated off from FC ownership to release private-sector capital. Three current proposals, at Delamere (Cheshire), Fineshade (Northants) and in the Forest of Dean, are concerning local people. All it takes is a Minister, or Defra official, to say 'we've leased the land to them, it's nothing to do with us' and the privatisation and forest sales issue will blow up again, compromising many of the genuine business opportunities that could develop in the FC forests.

If Government is not careful it could end up in a situation where it is blamed whenever anything goes wrong, and FC gets the credit when things go well.

Regardless of opposition, Defra proposed to produce draft legislation which would have had a minimal chance of success – and, as a result, may well have been watered down to nothing more than a transfer of ownership from the Secretary of State to the new FC estate management body, and provision for some additional commercial powers.

Chapter 12: Future Forests

However, it emerged that Defra were consulting FC staff on the proposals, and, under pressure, it agreed to extend the consultation to an invited range of organisations and individuals – a list which this time was fair and open, gathering in not just the insider 'establishment'.

The results were not a surprise: consultees said 'this has nothing to do with what the Panel recommended, and we won't support it'. Another long silence, a change of Minister, and in December 2013, the *Woodland Policy Enabling Programme – Update* was published. Over Dan Rogerson's name, it 'emphasises the Government's complete commitment to establishing a new, operationally independent, public body to own and manage the Public Forest Estate (PFE) for the benefit of people, nature and the economy.' It also published many of the responses received by the consultation, but still no detail on what the Government actually proposes to do.

A month later on 29th January 2014 it was followed by a paper to the England National Forestry Forum which went further in stating the government's position, reverting emphatically to the Panel recommendations: a truly independent body, a genuine focus on the triple bottom line, rather than the previous bias towards making money, commitment to adequate funding for public benefit delivery and a Charter as proposed by the IFP.

This is a massive step forward, a change of heart, and a hint that at last there is a single government position to concluding the issue – and removing the risk of forest sales blowing up for the Conservatives as the general election approaches. However, it is what happens next that matters and there are two issues:

Will the positive sentiments be carried through honestly to the detail of legislation, or will there be further attempts to slip in undermining measures?

And will it actually happen?

There is a lot to do and time is running out. There is quite clearly a voice within government cautioning 'do nothing – it'll be OK, we'll get away with it'. As Defra is a department expert in procrastination and delay, and many of the civil servants who felt the full pain of the original opposition to the sales proposals have moved on, there is a real risk the do nothing point of view will prevail. It is not helped by the fact that, with a single exception, Defra has lost every single battle over forestry policy, going right back to its original attempt to take over forestry policy from FC in 2005.

The flip side is that the chances are that forestry will blow up again as an issue before the election and, even failing that, it is a topic which, embarrassingly, comes up every time the Government's 'U-turns' are listed. The Conservatives have a real interest in ensuring forestry does not make it to the hustings. It **can** be done: the proposals on the table, developed into legislation that reflects both their letter and spirit could, I believe, be translated into law quickly and with widespread support.

What might that look like? For me, the issue breaks out simply into two issues: Governance and Resources.

On Governance, the key is that the Board must be constituted so that it places the interests of the forests first and not any sectoral, financial or political interest. Achieving that is far from easy, depending on an appointment system that spreads influence across everyone with an interest in the forest. There are some possible models within forestry: both the Forestry Commissioners and the Verderers of the New Forest have combined official appointments with seats for particular interests – for example, for the Forestry Commissioners, seats on the board nominated by the timber industry, forestry trade unions and the environment.

The Commissioners include executives – full time, salaried staff – alongside non-executives, the Verderers do not, but the Verderers do also include directly elected representatives of the local population (rather than nominated Local Authority councillors, as on National Park boards).

I would see a combination of some or all of these options going to make up a Board which would put the forest first. I have no objection to the Secretary of State appointing the Chair: it makes

Chapter 12: Future Forests

sense as a direct link to national democratic politics. Boards with executive representation work better in my experience; and nominated seats, however that nomination is carried out, guard against special interests dominating – as the various interests will always have different, and non party political, objectives. For local representation, direct election has a considerable attraction, even if it might be quite hard to implement. I have heard that options along these lines are under discussion within Defra.

I have also heard there may be similar positive discussions around resources. Key to a properly resourced future forest estate is the acceptance that it is a mix of genuine business, funded by trading, and public benefit delivery that cannot be financed from income: in the past it was suggested that the estate, as a 'business', should break even. By my calculation that would be equivalent to a 30% profit on operating revenue. Now, I understand, serious discussions are looking at how that public benefit might be funded, with the suggestion that there should be a hard contract (not the woolly, internal, service-level agreement normal within government departments) for FC to be funded to deliver specified public benefits. FC would positively welcome clear, deliverable targets set at a competitive level of return: there is nothing FC staff welcome more than a clear delivery challenge, nothing they resent more than the suggestion that government money is a subsidy or a loss.

Some benefits are easy to define: heathland management, for example, which is pure cost. It is also easy to cost because there are 'standard costs' to government both from their own agency, Natural England, and from funding to charities and private owners through schemes such as Higher Level Stewardship. A suggested figure of £22 million per annum would be the right base for a viable future forest estate – on the one hand enough to deliver, on the other still a considerable saving to government against standard costs. FC's lower costs are achievable partly through scale and partly through efficient use of resources honed through years of depressed timber prices.

The linked proposal that FC should pay a dividend to the government above set levels of profitability will, I am sure, worry some forest supporters. As long as it is a real 'commercial' dividend as paid to shareholders, where the needs of the business are taken into account, and not simply a Treasury cash grab, I am not too concerned – in fact, I see positive benefits. Hard though it is to imagine, I do believe we could see a real rise in timber values and there are a lot more opportunities to make money on the people side of the business. It would serve the estate as badly to be extravagantly profitable whilst still drawing taxpayers' money as it would to be bankrupt. A dividend will also check the inevitable nibbling away at the money for public benefit which I suspect will start even before the deal is signed and sealed!

There are real hints that Defra is 'getting it' and I could not applaud that more warmly. I just hope it will stick; there are so many obstacles, not least continuing budget cuts and the new development of the aftermath of the flooding still in progress as I write. It is the lack of detail, the temptation to talk but not do that means my conclusion still has to be that:

'The Forests are not safe – Yet'

I fervently hope that by the time this book is published it will be possible to say 'safe in their hands': it can be done, with leadership from Owen Paterson and Dan Rogerson. It is what the people who care want, and politically there is little to lose and much to gain – not least avoiding the near certainty of this issue exploding again close to the General Election in 2015.

Whilst all this has been going on around the future of the forest estate there have been three other major events, which I will outline below.

Government agencies are routinely reviewed every three years – the triennial review. Often they are little more than routine. However, the review that got under way as the forest sales story unfolded was clearly out for blood: there was going to be an

Chapter 12: Future Forests

amalgamation of at least two of the agencies under review and, whilst it was meant to be about the Environment Agency and Natural England, it became clear that Forest Services (the new name for the Forestry Authority – the advice, grants and regulatory arm of FC) was the preferred target which was logical because, without the estate, it was too small to stand alone and surely, under cover of the debate on the estate, too small to attract much attention. Administrative changes like this are a favourite within government – creating the illusion of action without doing anything real, and slowing or halting serious business. That was what happened with this review. Its importance was rapidly inflated into an excuse for slowing action in other areas; however, as it grew so too did the opposition. With its developing ability to create unlikely alliances, Defra found itself facing not only the forestry sector and the public forest protestors but now, too, the Woodland Trust.

The argument was simple and the case strong: small bodies absorbed into larger ones lose their influence, and the objectors saw the small, thin, voice of forestry and woodlands within government completely silenced.

The case is overwhelming: under the previous government the Countryside Agency's access and rural communities agenda was virtually lost when Natural England was formed and under the present government the environment part of Defra – junior partner to the agricultural Ministry of Agriculture, Fisheries and Food (MAFF) when the new ministry was formed – has declined through cuts and loss of influence. Forest Services – and Natural England – survived; there were no amalgamations and just as the forest sales fiasco saved the Forestry Commission, as I write the winter flooding has raised questions over the resourcing, and importance, of the Environment Agency.

Since then the alliance has hardened further with RSPB joining the fray at full force as they realise that the failure to resolve and develop the Government's efforts for woodlands guarantees the continuing decline of many woodland birds.

Proof of the risks to forestry had Forest Services been lost came quickly: while forestry was diverted by administrative wranglings, planners for the interim arrangements between the end of one European Regional Development Programme (under the Common Agricultural Policy; CAP) missed forestry grants for new planting, and it emerged there would be two years with no grants whatsoever. That would mean the permanent loss of the approximately 6,000 hectares of new woodland that would, on average, be planted over two years. This, again, was in sharp contrast to the Panel's call for an increase in woodland planting. Once again there was a vigorous response from foresters and the Woodland Trust, one of the biggest planters in England, resulting in interim funding being restored.

There was a particular irony in this because the uncertainties of planting, and the resulting impact on the domestic tree nursery trade, was central to the other major event: the discovery of the devastating new disease of Ash, *Chalara fraxinea*, in the UK. *Chalara* has been moving across Europe from the east and has largely wiped out Ash in Denmark. It was first found on newly planted trees of British (seed) origin which had, however, been raised in Dutch nurseries. It became clear that infected trees were all over the UK in new planting and nurseries, but that the disease had also arrived naturally, with a cluster of outbreaks in mature woodland in East Anglia. There is no doubt that the arrival on young nursery stock was a failure for both government and the forestry sector in the past.

However, the Government responded with commendable speed and decision, and Owen Paterson showed real leadership in pulling together government agencies and the forestry sector. Key to the effective response, and of great significance for the wider forestry scene, he had at his shoulder Defra Chief Scientist, Ian Boyd. Faced with an invasive disease, his fundamental understanding of biological processes was more important than detailed forestry knowledge.

An effective action plan, with the whole FC turned out into the countryside to undertake an instant survey, backed up by DNA

Chapter 12: Future Forests

analysis by the Food and Environment Research Agency (FERA) scientists, quickly established the true scale of the problem. Movement of potentially infected Ash within the UK was halted, followed quickly by a ban on imports. Yes, it was closing the stable door on a predictable problem – reflecting the lowly position of forestry in the Government's pecking order, but that was a long-term issue. The short-term response was more effective and it does prove that Defra – and government – can get it right.

Looking to the forests of the future, knowledge and expertise looms ever larger, more so than the more obvious question of money. Whether Defra – and government more widely – is able to 'get it', to understand how to put together the pieces of the complex and challenging jigsaw that is our forests, and our countryside, becomes increasingly important.

I am convinced we are now in a position to solve many demanding problems facing England and save money at the same time. I am also convinced that harnessing expertise and introducing new thinking, beyond the assumptions and institutions that may be a bigger barrier to progress than the real, physical world, is a pivotal issue.

Looking back I am overawed by the power of the multi-disciplinary teams I worked with: for brown field restoration, covering everything from the microscopic science of soil structure through practical tree planting and civil engineering to biodiversity, aesthetic design and working with local communities. This is a message that has been driven home for me through working with other bodies that do not have the benefit of that well-developed team and infrastructure of expertise.

In contrast, however, since Defra decided it should lead on forestry policy in 2005 it has struggled constantly and disastrously. Its experience has seen the limits of a generalist civil service stretched beyond breaking point and, whilst ministers must take responsibility for their own stupidities, I feel very sympathetic towards civil service colleagues who have been caught in the cross fire and required to advise on issues way beyond their expertise.

Forest Vision

The work around the Independent Forestry Panel, which must have cost over £1m, built a real foundation of knowledge amongst panel members and their supporting civil servants. With the papers, consultee inputs and field visits, the Panel must have been close to a taught Master's degree in contemporary forest management. At last, I hoped, Defra had the knowledge base it needed to start participating in real forest policy decision-making. Not so. Every member of the forestry team was posted to new, unrelated jobs as soon as the Panel reported. It may even have been worse than just wasting this priceless body of expertise: it is rumoured that staff had become too favourable to forestry as they had grown to understand it. Surely it is time for the Government and the department to consider whether it is they, not the rest of their fellow citizens in the wider world, that have got it wrong?

The above has been particularly clear in the dealings with the community, protestors, whatever the people opposed to the sell-off should be called: the people who objected who were not inside the establishment tent as the forest sales issue broke. The Government reaction has been a strange combination of fear, respect and contempt. Defra people have been commendably anxious to understand the spectacular social media campaign run through the Save our Woods website and associated Facebook and Twitter by Hen Anderson. They have struggled to recognise that people such as Rich Daniels, Chair of Forest of Dean's HOOF (Hands off Our Forest) and Anne Mason of Friends of Thetford Forest Park actually know more about forestry, their forests and their forest communities than anyone in central government.

The suggestion of community representation on the Board of the new organisation to run the public forests was met with a contemptuous: 'oh they'll only want to talk about their local footpaths'. Again, I realise how lucky I – and my FC colleagues – are by comparison: I cut my teeth in village halls in my mid-30s, going out from Bristol to support Forest Districts where local disputes had got out of hand. In the Forest of Dean and the New Forest there is at

Chapter 12: Future Forests

least one big dispute and many little ones on the go every single day; Rich and I can sit down together, have a good argument about what FC is doing (I am still defending them!) and go away understanding and respecting each other's positions; but I understand completely how difficult it is for officials who have never had this sort of dealing and know a good deal less than the people to whom they are talking. Further, it has not helped that community representatives have refused to swallow the attempts at traditional government 'consultation' involving bringing people together, telling them what is going to happen and then claiming that 'the community has been consulted'.

This is a much bigger issue than just forest sales. There is a growing pattern of the community effectively blocking major – and, were they better executed, potentially desirable – initiatives such as GM crops, wind farms, HS2, fracking. All have come up hard against a sceptical public and all have something in common which makes them particularly significant and different: they are not, which was also the case with the forest sales protest, defined by party politics. Ministers suggesting that objectors are 'wicked' or 'irrational' is probably not quite the right way to go about bringing people round. Neither will blowing away regulations solve the problem: in every case, badly thought through plans are trying to hide behind legislation and the planning system and it simply is not working. It is time for a re-think on how we do this sort of government and the Forestry Commission approach is probably a good place to start.

Many of the most forceful supporters of the Forestry Commission have been converts: environmentalists who were, rightly, equally vigorous opponents of FC in the 1980s. Looking to the future, it is important to recognise just how different FC really is from the attitude within government betrayed by the endless, unqualified references to it becoming 'more commercial'. Reporting on its targets, FC in 2013 had 634 private businesses operating on the public forest estate in England. Some of that is private business replacing public, for example harvesting timber and planting trees, but much – almost all the recreation such as cycling hire and shops – is new. It is economic growth: It is about making the public asset of the land work harder for the economy and for the visitors to the forest. Because FC provides the setting – the land – and often operates low fixed rent plus percentage of turnover, many of those businesses are small and local, and they reflect my ambition: to shrink the state not through crude cuts, but through helping the private sector grow the economy.

FC is efficient: in 2013 the public forest estate cost the taxpayer £63.33 per hectare, compared to the £200/ha paid to lowland farmland under The Single Farm Payment. As a result of the crash in timber prices most of the FC's capital investment over the past 15 years has come from third-party sources and was won against competition. Peaking at £15m in a year, FC external funding was way ahead of the much bigger fellow Defra agencies, the Environment Agency and Natural England. In contrast to the norm in government, where massive overruns are common, FC built a dozen new forest centres without a single significant overrun: there was simply no money to pay for one, and, unlike when wider government pleas poverty, suppliers believed us.

So, again suggesting that Defra really is 'getting it', the language in the 29th January statement has shifted from 'be more commercial' to 'build on the strengths of Forest Enterprise England' and I am hearing rumours of FC increasingly being seen, once again, as an exemplar.

Into the Future

This leads us on into the future. In a throwback to the 19th century, the public forest estate, and the FC, is generally viewed as a large chunk of hard assets – land. With the profligacy towards skills and expertise discussed above, government has attached no value to the expertise of the management organisation. This is a long, long way from a 21st century where knowledge is everything, so that digital

Chapter 12: Future Forests

and media companies with no hard assets whatsoever can be worth billions of pounds. Looking over the horizon, is FC actually worth more for its expertise – the intellectual property involved in turning science into action on the ground – than the land ? Companies like the huge US oil services business Halliburton are valued for their ability to co-ordinate, plan and deliver complex solutions. FC is not much different, with the peri-urban programme probably the clearest example, where for every £1 it spent it probably saved the taxpayer another £1 compared to the next best supplier.

As I write the flooding crisis is hopefully (but it is still raining) at its peak. For the first time in a generation the reality that we can manage, but cannot control, our environment is dawning. The debate over dredging the Somerset Levels is seminal: not between 'dredge' against 'don't dredge', but rather dredging as the one and only solution against dredging as one part of a wider solution. I was amazed to hear Owen Paterson saying '(tree) planting, SUDS (sustainable urban drainage systems) ….' rather than simply the politically easy – and politically, if not monetarily, cheap – 'we'll dredge' when he visited the Somerset Levels: again he had clearly been listening to his advisers.

This is the pattern of the debate about wider landuse. The National Farmers Union (NFU) all-out campaign for food security sharpens the choice between single purpose landuse and the multipurpose, multi-benefit, approach of modern forestry. Food security is easy to sell – especially compared to the ill-chosen, cliquey concepts of biodiversity or ecosystem services. It draws on over 60 years of policy assumptions going back to the 1947 Agriculture Act. It is consistent with the assumption that flood protection is about heavy engineering – dredging, concrete walls, and sluices.

Single-purpose management delivers a lot of just one product from each area of land and, in the process, frequently also delivers negative downstream consequences: quite literally in the case of single-purpose agriculture, where the huge government-funded land drainage campaigns of the '60s and '70s have speeded water runoff in vulnerable river catchments such as the Thames and Severn.

Single-purpose management is going to save us with one simple solution, we are told: all-out farming will feed us, fracking or nuclear will keep us warm – each lobby shouting hard for its unique place in the sun. Forestry will not. There is not enough space in the UK to provide for all our timber needs or more than a fraction of our energy; and to pretend forestry can on its own solve issues of urbanisation, childhood obesity and flooding is patently absurd. It can, however, make a significant contribution to every one of those issues – unlike single-purpose intensive farming, wind farms or so many other simple, limited solutions.

There is now a very clear choice: The public forests, and the way they have been managed over the past 20 years, are the clearest example of considered land management for multiple objectives. Of course others are doing it but usually with a single objective uppermost, and when the debate gets going they tend to revert to their sectoral objectives – so nature conservation still struggles conceptually (though often not in practice) with people on nature reserves and most interests failing to recruit others to converging outcomes. The whole forest sales issue is already building bridges between the forestry and conservation sectors – a divide FC was already straddling, if sometimes uncomfortably.

Multi-purpose landuse is complicated – an orchestra, compared to the simple, brazen, trumpet of single-purpose use. There is always a demand for a 'lead objective', and often there will be one, but even if there is, it may well disappear behind another, more visible one: how many of the wise academics who walk and talk on Oxford's famous Port Meadow realise how important it is in buffering the city from flooding? How many mountain-bikers stop to consider the timber industry as they struggle, mud splashed, through Grizedale Forest? The effort and thought that has turned rigid plantations into increasingly attractive and natural-looking landscapes is simply taken for granted.

Chapter 12: Future Forests

Foresters are in favour of trees, and they have a long track record of saying 'we want more trees' and then thinking of a good reason. Even the Panel's proposal that England should increase its tree cover from 10 to 15% falls into this trap.

I want to go back to fundamentals – the Eftec 'ranking' for the different values of trees and forests – and look at the outcomes that can be achieved for society as a whole in England from future forests.

Flooding is topical and a good place to start. Flooding is about people. It is not, as has been suggested, a town versus country issue: the town will always win, but rather than trashing the country, the wider landscape must be recruited – and paid – to provide flood control to urban areas. Flooding illustrates perfectly why single solution approaches do not work, and why giving absolute priority to food and farming is flawed: food and timber are freely traded around the world, flooding is here and now, in specific places in England and can only be tackled right there. Flooding is not just about absolute amounts of water but also how fast they travel and, as a result, how high they rise in any part of the catchment.

Landuse has exacerbated flooding: beyond the removal of trees (for which we can probably blame the Romans!), the drainage campaign of the '50s to '70s hastened water even faster off the land by installing under field drainage. Large areas of low-lying meadow were converted to arable and farming systems intolerant of flooding, in contrast to old permanent pasture. Contrary to popular belief, it seems to be the middle reaches rather than the headwaters where the peak flows that do the damage in flooding can be reduced, water held back to drain away after the crisis has passed. Grassland planned for flooding, the direction of water to places it will do less harm, gentle engineering to direct and check water and trees which, through greater friction slow water better than open land, should all be components of more natural flood defences: and hard engineering must continue to play a part; it is not the all-or-nothing of traditional single-purpose landuse. That is key to future thinking.

It means landuse change – and tree planting – on a scale unprecedented since the original FC afforestation, so, the obvious question is how to pay for it? Quite simply, we already are paying and will have to pay more if we continue down the present single-objective landuse track. My question is the opposite: what could we save? The Government's Foresight Review of flooding predicted costs rising as high as £40 billion per annum under some climate-change scenarios! The 2007 summer floods cost the economy roughly the same as the whole government subsidy to farming and forestry for the year and it looks as if the winter 2013-14 floods could well equal or exceed the 2007 costs. That subsidy, at roughly £3 billion, is both a lot of money and a huge barrier: any change has to 'buy out' the value of agricultural subsidy, at least doubling land values and meaning that any new use competes only after climbing a mountain rather than on a level playing field. Spending on flooding may be £800 million and another £800 million goes on cleaning pollution, mostly runoff from intensive farmland, from our drinking water. The money is there: it is our human institutions which stop it going where it is needed – not geography, climate or ecology.

Prioritising land for flood defence would eat into agricultural land but how important is that really? Firstly, whilst agriculture lays claim to every square inch of the landscape, in the nature of multi-purpose landuse flood defence would use only a limited area. Secondly, production of commodities would not be lost, with lower output grazing and timber production as subsidiary uses. Thirdly, although the first priority is flood defence, what other benefits could the land deliver?

Eftec argues that woods and trees in and around our towns and cities deliver the greatest benefits, of which flood management may be just one. There is growing support for trees in our towns and cities, for the way they soften the concrete jungle as much as for their practical functionality in providing shade, air quality and natural 'air conditioning'. Again, there is more to trees than reductionist economics can easily describe. They are there with us, a big

Chapter 12: Future Forests

presence, valued less than our buildings but often transforming urban landscapes. However, on top of this established and growing recognition of value within our towns and cities there it is an undiscovered land that I believe is equally important: the space in which we set our towns and cities, the land surrounding them and what it does for people and their environment.

Too many green belts, the land reserved by the planning system to limit urban sprawl are anything but, polluted by activities like mineral extraction and land fill with waste, and out in the country intensive farmland sweeps right up to the last larch lap fence of small towns, which often have less internal green space than big cities. There is talk now of new 'garden cities'; but they eat space and embed the car, Milton Keynes style, as the only viable means of transport. In contrast, the high density of recent urban development has a hidden benefit: it means people can be closer to the edge, to a garden for everyone around the town, rather than everyone with a tiny garden. Richard Rogers put the services on the outside of the Pompidou Centre in Paris – a spectacular cat's cradle of brightly coloured pipework. Rather more subtly, why can we not put some of the services around rather than in our cities?

Why not surround new cities with community woodlands, nature reserves, reed beds and meadowland open to everyone? Behind the pretty facade this apparently lazy land will be working hard – a key weapon in the fight against obesity, getting children out from behind their computers and adults walking again. It will be absorbing the first shock of increasingly frequent floods, cleaning grey water through reed beds, reeds which, with wood from the forests, can be turned into carbon-lean fuel for the nearby town. People will cycle and walk to work on the comprehensive car-free network of walking and cycling routes, listening to Bitterns booming from the reeds, with woodpeckers and wildflowers for company, rather than concrete and steel.

Not the best time for big ideas? Well, government has opened the debate about planning and there is a need for change – so why can we not make it a positive change? At a fractious time, when national morale is low coming together around a vision of a brighter future is what leadership is about. That is especially so because Government's ambitions to make planning easier carries the risk that new house building will end up in the same impasse as other unpopular, poorly thought through, policies, blocked by lack of public support.

Again, money is there but blocked by our institutions: the cash flow through development is enormous and getting planning permission for a piece of land more like the lottery than a business deal: Why not 'dilute' development land with maybe 5 or 10 hectares of matching land for every developed hectare for 'green space' around the town? Would it matter if the million pound per hectare bonanza were reduced to one hundred thousand, just ten times rather than one hundred times more than agricultural value? It is already happening – for example, with Peterborough's Hampton development where a large area of land was left undeveloped as part of the planning deal but, sadly, without any strong vision for its future. The story of the northwest makes the point of how important creating great environments could be for our future economic health, as well as our physical health.

This is the new woodland culture the Panel advocates; and it is coming up from the grassroots as much as down from government: the local groups protecting and volunteering to look after local land. Small woods are a problem for big organisations – as much for The Woodland Trust as they have grown bigger as for FC. The Tree Council's Tree Wardens are one way of linking people to their trees. There is a growing movement for traditional management, hand crafting traditional furniture and buildings; notably by people such as Mike Abbot, author, green woodworker, teacher and champion, and Gudrun Leitz who hand-turned the balustrades for the Globe Theatre in London. Paul Hayden now runs a dozen green woodwork chair-making courses a year in the magnificent Oak-framed Westonbirt craft shelter built by master timber framer Henry

Chapter 12: Future Forests

Russell, who also teaches as he builds. Small woodlands are sold by Woodlands for Sale, and supported by new organisations such as the Small Woods Association and the *Living Woods* and *Tree News* magazines. Professional foresters can be a bit confused – 'but there aren't jobs for all the people being trained' – and miss the point completely: the beauty and excitement of spending a week somewhere like Westonbirt creating a chair from green wood in a stunning woodland glade, to take home and remember, the new skills, new friends and that pause in a busy urban life.

Leading on from people's increasing engagement with trees, it is easy to slip into talking about trees and woodlands simply as a tool. Current economic thinking pushes that way, as it pushes towards simplification: that economists have difficulty measuring the complexity of multi-purpose systems can undermine their apparent viability. But, as Oliver Rackham points out, trees are wildlife in their own right, not just places for other creatures to live. They have an intrinsic value of their own and a wood, even a planted wood, is more than a neat field of wheat. Stepping into a wood from the open means re-joining nature: in the light and shade people and animals can hide. A Roe deer drifts across a patch of sunlight and simply disappears. Some beauty is glaringly obvious such as a vibrant carpet of bluebells, but much is hidden: a Pied Flycatcher darting into its nest hole, the microscopic fungi so vital to the forest cycle, lichens clinging to a giant old oak high in the forest canopy. That single old Oak is in itself a marvel: one of the few natural things far bigger and far older than us humans and our creations, and a complex tower block of life, a whole functioning ecosystem extending out into the air we breathe, the water we drink and the houses we live in.

One big threat and one big opportunity hang over the future of our trees, woods and forests.

The threat is disease. Tree diseases have been multiplying at an alarming rate, some imported from abroad, some apparently through genetic mutation and some through changing climate. But uncertainty is ever present: what is the cause of *Dothistroma* – needle blight of pines – an endemic disease, no more than a curiosity 15 years ago, suddenly attacking Corsican Pine to the extent it is no longer a viable forestry tree? Just how fast will *Chalara* sweep through our Ash trees? It is possible to make some predictions: *Dothistroma* puts a question mark over whole forests – especially Thetford – as conifer timber producers, whilst *Phytophthora* looks like eliminating Larch as a forestry species for the foreseeable future. In native woodlands, my feeling is that dominant Ash may be replaced by the range of other species present but suppressed in many woods – Oak for example. But what if one of the diseases identified on Oak suddenly becomes more virulent? And, although the Ash may be replaced in woodland, forest inventory statistics show that the trees lost in open countryside from Dutch Elm Disease – hedge trees, field trees and parkland trees – were never replaced, lost forever from our landscape.

What can be done about it? 'Man in control of nature' won't work too well: treating trees with, for example, fungicides is difficult – due to the huge area of leaves and fungi getting under the bark, quite apart from wider environmental effects; so again it is a question of skill and expertise.

A key area, already under development in response to climate change, is alternative species and tree genetics. Westonbirt and Bedgebury Arboreta have come right back into their own, hosting a large number of professional forest visits over the last two years looking at possible new trees for British forestry as well as for our streets and gardens. At last the threat of imports is being taken seriously; and the FC successfully contained an occurrence of the fearsome Asian Long Horn Beetle.

The opportunity is carbon. Rated above both timber and biodiversity in the Eftec study, carbon still does not have a formal cash value in the UK. It is, however, a part of government environmental and energy accounting under international treaties and it is traded voluntarily by private companies. FC has produced a carbon code

Chapter 12: Future Forests

as an assurance to investors that they are getting what they are paying for in an emerging market that has already seen its fair share of sharks. Formal carbon trading, backed by cash, could transform forestry – and tree planting – in the UK.

Even without carbon, the outlook for timber has changed dramatically. It remains vital to forestry because whilst the economic value of flood prevention, trees around towns and carbon capture may be huge, at the moment that value does not often translate into the hard cash needed to run a forestry business.

The Renewable Heat Incentive does do just that and is at the heart of a resurgence in a wood and timber sector brought to its knees by cripplingly low timber values. What is becoming clearer is that forestry had its recession early – and long – from the timber price crash in 1996 to 2006 as wood energy started to take hold. Two other factors have been important: the first is the pull from the East, the prospect that demand from China is underpinning real timber values on the world market. There have been false dawns before and that theory needs qualifying with the fact that Europe as a whole, not just the UK, is still undercutting its timber resource. However, the East does seem to have absorbed new capacity coming on stream in Eastern European EU accession states which would otherwise have headed west to lower UK prices.

The second, and more concrete factor, which made forestry very counter-cyclical during the 2008 crash, is the 25% drop in the value of the pound against the Euro, making imports from Europe massively more expensive and allowing domestic timber to grab more and more of the critical construction sector. Forest Enterprise's timber income has topped £30 million from its low of £17.5m, but still way off the 1996 peak of £38m, even without taking 17 years' inflation into account. In the longer term, whilst energy may not inflate prices for higher-use wood like construction, it must very clearly underpin the value of lower value wood because European demand for energy is effectively infinite in forestry terms and at best UK production can only supply a tiny proportion of our needs.

The recession has had a further impact, cushioning the pain of low returns from day to day forestry business: capital has flown towards the safety of hard assets such as land and sales values for forests has rocketed, perhaps helped a little by the high profile the sales fiasco has given forestry. In popular lowland areas prices are scarcely behind agricultural land and the extra value of attractive, mixed, estates to rich lifestyle purchasers has been reinforced.

Fortunately, the forest industry has been able to grow despite government's distraction over the future of FC. However, there's little doubt that opportunities have been lost through the failure to focus hard on supporting this rapidly developing market.

There is a big and looming risk here: despite rising prices, there is market failure in bringing woods into management. Owners who have not managed for decades are not in touch with rising prices and do not have the skills to manage their woods. Lack of timber could knock out existing businesses and leave new wood-energy users without supply. Both the actual and reputational damage to forestry could be severe; and this is the key pivot point where government needs to act – not alone, but alongside private- and third-sector organisations including the Institute of Chartered Foresters, the Royal Forestry Society and Confor. This is where Forest Services – and the forestry profession – become vital, in ensuring the wood comes to the market and from good, sustainable management. There are real concerns that even as Forest Services engage owners, the practical skills may not be out there amongst the forestry sector.

It all comes back, again, to skills: doing what FC does is not about learning by rote. Each new wood, each wood brought back into management, is a unique challenge, and it is the professional planner, determining what is going to happen in that wood, who is crucial. Are the skills there to get the best out of the opportunities, to recognise and incorporate history, to understand and balance wildlife and heritage values with economic timber harvesting? If not, the whole sector is at threat because mistakes undermine everyone,

Chapter 12: Future Forests

however good and however distant from the action, as the 'Flow Country' proved.

That skill applies equally to biodiversity. There is such a huge opportunity in the future forests. In almost every other case it is human activity that is damaging our wildlife. Only in the neglected woods is it lack of activity that is the problem. This is one place where we can reverse the decline in biodiversity in the wider environment, not just on nature reserves. The skills are already there: managed woodlands already do better for many threatened species, especially the iconic and popular early succession species ranging from Bluebell through Nightingale to Dormouse. We must tackle the nervousness in the NGOs through new partnerships between foresters and conservationists, setting out not to blame and misunderstand but to do the work needed to get results for everyone. It is perhaps ironic that opposing Defra has created some unlikely new relationships which I do hope will flourish.

From my point of view, new woodlands also open up the opportunity to re-create more habitat such as lowland heath. There is no case for reducing England's already skimpy forest area, but with significant new woodland planted for new benefits there would be an argument for moving trees off other habitats – a really positive biodiversity offsetting. However, whilst conservationists often talk 'landscape scale', all too often that reverts to rather narrow views on habitat; so if big changes are to happen there will need to be an upping of the game to create real, new, landscapes, not just another chunk of restored heath.

Illustrating how a new, outcome-driven approach to landuse could work is an idea proposed for the Sherwood Forest area but never implemented. Clipstone Forest sits on an important aquifer. Trees use more water than the heathland the forest was planted on – but at least the water flowing through the forest is pristinely clean. Not so the water from the pig farms surrounding the forest and polluting the aquifer. So why not move the forest out onto the pig farming land, as a ring round open heathland in the middle, thus stopping the pollution and increasing yield from the aquifer? Unlike the aquifer, the pigs could move to somewhere else. The simple answer is the huge cost where water would have to buy out farming. It is the same for the much-wider pollution from farming more generally, as illustrated by the Sherwood case, because the pure water wasn't for local people: no, it is piped across to East Anglia to dilute drinking water with too high a nitrate level from local intensive farming!

Now is the time to stand back to look at how scarce space is best used, and what we really need to buy with all the money already pouring into the countryside for today's urgent needs. It is not an 'either/or' as the intensive farming lobby would like to portray it: imagine what you could do with 500,000 hectares, new woodlands, new habitats, flood control, new landscapes around towns. It is more than two times the single biggest landholding in England, the public forests; and yet it is only 5% of our land surface and, in agricultural terms, UK food output has changed (usually upwards) by more than 5% in most decades since 1940.

In terms of food security it is no more than noise in the system. Farmers are understandably nervous of change, especially with the fickleness of any government support other than the CAP. It is vital, and something about which I feel passionately, that land managers are paid for the goods they deliver for society, not as subsidy but as payment for services – just as is hopefully being discussed for the future funding of public benefits delivered by the public forests. Would it not be better and fairer down on the Somerset Levels for farmers to be paid to hold water on their land? Would anyone whose house has been flooded be anything other than grateful?

Once trees are part of the new landuse, whatever their primary purpose, good design can deliver a whole range of further benefits: there is no place in our crowded country for more crude, single-species, single-purpose plantations; in the lowlands even less so than in the uplands. All tree planting should aim to look good and, even if dominated by faster growing non-natives, should

Chapter 12: Future Forests

always include native trees and – equally important – include open space with any area of existing biodiversity value, like unimproved wet grassland preserved and managed with care. The woods, which might be there first and foremost to protect homes from flooding, will produce timber for energy and construction and the attractive, beautifully designed woods will be new countryside for all to enjoy, new green space for people. In time that will seem to be the most important value – only when the storm surges will people be reminded of the main reason the trees were originally planted!

The Independent Panel's call for a new woodland culture is seminal: it is hugely important, because, with the learning, the appreciation, the enjoyment of our trees, woods and forests comes, first, awareness, and beyond that, the sort of imaginative new ways of doing things I am trying to communicate here, and throughout this book.

It is indeed a green and pleasant land in which we are privileged to live here in England. Let us keep it that way, and keep it prosperous on a rapidly changing world stage by making it a place in which people choose to live and work. I am proud that through the developments in forestry over the last 30 years, a new model for landuse has been created; and the exemplars of how we can do new and different things are already there, visible for anyone who is prepared to look. We can build resilience into our trees, our landscape and our towns and cities for an unpredictable future. However, I am convinced we can go further: creating beautiful places to live, actually winding back the risk of a country that feels ever more crowded. Increasingly, blasting the way through problems with money and heavy engineering looks impossible. It is the skill to combine the best of science, the best of beauty and practical delivery to liberate imagination to do better than simply solve our problems, to go further, to fly higher.

So many of our barriers we have built ourselves and can just as easily remove. Looking back to the past and the problems that always come to the front of my mind, I'm staggered by how far and how fast the forests, the people who manage them and the people who enjoy and love them have come. So many of the barriers were set up by people and preserved through culture, not necessity, and the challenge is to break down those barriers to open the doors to the future. I do have faith in the future – we really can do better for Britain.

Glossary

38 Degrees Novel internet campaigning organisation, with over a million members; the petition over forest sales which reached 530,000 signatures did as much to put the organisation on the map as it did to save the forests.

A&O (Ancient and Ornamental Woodland) Special designation of the ancient pasture woodland of The New Forest, which at over 4,000 hectares is the largest surviving area of pasture woodland in North West Europe.
acre Imperial area measure. Metric hectares are now generally used in forestry. (I acre = 0.404 hectares)
allowable cut The amount of timber which can be cut to sustain the long-term timber production of the forest.
apical track shoes Very wide tracks for crawler tractors with cleats with a rounded, as opposed to the normal vertical, profile to avoid breaking through soft surfaces. Developed for ploughing and draining very soft, wet sites.
aquifer Water bearing geological strata, from which water may be abstracted.
arboretum A botanical collection of trees.
ASNW (Ancient Semi-Natural Woodland) Ancient woodland where the tree species are native to the site. The 'semi-natural' recognises that virtually all woods in Britain have been modified by man and most have been heavily managed for centuries, but none the less retain significant natural elements, especially the slow-spreading ground flora species that characterise ancient woodland.
AW (Ancient Woodland) Woodland with a long history, in theory possibly stretching back to the wild wood before man's intervention, in practice woodland where there is evidence of presence prior to 1600.

'Big Society' A political concept of community engagement developed by David Cameron as he became prime Minister, but which quickly faded from the political scene.
brownfield Land previously developed for housing, industry or extraction, often with damaged or polluted soils.
BTO (British Trust for Ornithology) Bird research charity based around fieldwork by volunteer ornithologists – an exemplar of 'citizen science'.

CAP (Common Agricultural Policy) The EU policy supporting agriculture including paying large subsidies to EU farmers.
CC/CA (Countryside Commission/Countryside Agency) Government agency for landscape, access and the countryside, amalgamated into Natural England (NE).
CCF (Continuous Cover Forestry) A small-scale system where a site is never clear felled, with new growth being promoted in small groups, or even individual trees,

by careful management of the larger trees. A low-impact system which retains forest cover but which may limit the use of light-demanding species such as Oak.
CLA (Country Landowners Association, now Country Land and Business Association) Representative body for landowners.
clear fell Where all the trees on the site are felled for timber at once, generally followed by replanting. By far the dominant silvicultural system in UK forestry.
CMF (Capital Modernisation Fund) A Treasury Fund introduced in the early 2000s to promote new solutions through capital spending.
Common Ground A charitable organisation promoting local character and traditions in the countryside.
Confor Representative body for forestry and the forest industries.
conservancy Term used for regional forest management units, originally for all FC activities, more recently for Forestry Authority/ Forest Services regions.
coppice Ancient silvicultural system where trees are cut off at the base and regenerate naturally by producing new shoots: most native trees regenerate this way, but few conifers. Regrowth must be protected from browsing animals.
CRoW (Countryside and Rights of Way Act) Passed in 2000, this act gave open access to 'unenclosed countryside' and the ability to 'dedicate' other land for open access. The whole Forestry Commission freehold estate is dedicated.
cubic metres The measure used for timber, roughly equivalent to a metric tonne.

Dafs (Department of Agriculture and Fisheries for Scotland) Pre-devolution rural Ministry for Scotland.
DCLG (Department of Communities and Local Government) Local Government Ministry succeeding ODPM in 2006.
DECC (Department of Energy and Climate Change) Formed in 2008, taking over energy and the new topic of Climate Change.
deer lawns Open areas selected by wildlife rangers to attract deer and facilitate shooting to control populations and therefore damage to trees.
Defra (Department for the Environment, Food and Rural Affairs) Formed from MAFF and the wildlife and countryside sections of DETR, responsible for agriculture, fisheries, forestry and wider rural policy.
delimbing Cutting the branches off the tree after felling.
DETR (Department of Environment and Transport and the Regions) Formed in 1997, the local Government and Environment Ministry, split into ODPM, Defra and Transport in 2001.

Eftec (Economics for the Environment Consultancy) A London based consulting company specialising in environmental economics
EN (English Nature) The Government nature conservation agency in England which succeeded NCC and was then amalgamated into Natural England (NE).
EU Birds Directive EU bird-protection directive, implemented through the SPA land designation.

Glossary

EU Habitats Directive EU habitat protection directive, implemented through the SAC designation.
EU LIFE The EU funding programme to support management of sites designated as SAC and SPA.
FA (Forestry Authority) The regulatory and grants arm of FC following the split into two separate organisations in 1992.
FC (Forestry Commission) The government forestry body responsible for managing the national forests, regulation and grant aid to private forestry and for forest research. Used in this book as an overarching name, especially for national policy, and also for the nationally owned forests alongside Forest Enterprise.
FE (Forest Enterprise) The land-management body of the FC following the split into two separate organisations in 1992. A name which did not really stick, with public perception – eventually followed by FC itself – slipping back towards the well-known Forestry Commission name over time.
FERA (Food and Environment Research Agency) Defra's research agency for agriculture, environment and diseases of animals and plants.
'Flow Country' Name given to the extensive area of raised bogs and pools in Caithness and Sutherland in the far north of Scotland during the environmental dispute over conifer planting.
flushing When leaves or needles burst out of their buds in the spring. Trees should be planted well before flushing, whilst they are still dormant.
FMD (Foot and Mouth Disease) A very infectious disease of cattle, sheep and pigs, the last incidence of which closed the British countryside between January and May 2001.
Forest Holidays The business managing camping and forest cabin sites, now largely privatised through a joint venture in which FC retains a minority share. Forest Holidays uses the FC brand.
Forest Research The forestry research agency, which is the third arm of the FC.
freehold The freehold of land is the underlying right to the land. Freeholds may be leased to others, for a specified length of time and usually with conditions and there may be legal charges on a freehold – especially the common rights which are so important in the New Forest and constrain the Crown's (Forestry Commission) freehold.
FS (Forest Services) The current name of the regulatory and grants arm of the Forestry Commission.
FSC (Forestry Stewardship Council) An international forest certification body, which includes representatives of the forestry industry, environment and communities in its governance. The 'gold standard' of forest certification. In the UK it works to the UKWAS standard.
FWAG (Farming and Wildlife Advisory Group) A county-based conservation advisory service for farmers, run by farmers.

ginger group A group aimed at 'gingering up' government policy by monitoring, criticising and making suggestions for alternative approaches.

Green Belt Planning designation preventing urban sprawl by creating zones where development cannot take place around towns and cities. A successful, but largely negative measure, some green belts have been badly damaged by 'permitted development' such as mineral working and illegal activity including fly tipping and burnt-out cars.

green wood working Environmental yes, but actually refers to working in unseasoned wood cut straight from the forest. A very ancient traditional craft, the seasoning of the wood is used as part of the process, tightening joints as the wood dries. Best known is chair making, but green wood is also used in traditional Oak framing, the principle architectural method of the Middle Ages.

HCT (Herpetological Conservation Trust) Charity for the conservation of reptiles and amphibians.

hectare (Ha) Metric measure of area, now generally used in forestry (1 hectare = 2.47 acres).

HLF (Heritage Lottery Fund) The national lottery fund that grant aids countryside projects.

HLS (Higher Level Stewardship) Government programme under the CAP that grant aids management of the most environmentally important sites.

IFP (Independent Forestry Panel) Set up in 2011 by Defra after the U-turn on forest sales, the Panel was chaired by the Rev James Jones, Bishop of Liverpool, and reported a year later.

Intereg An EU programme that funds projects involving several EU countries, designed to foster co-operation and understanding across the EU.

IYE 1985 (International Year of the Environment 1985) A United Nations led initiative to promote the environment.

lawns Grassy areas, fertilised by winter floods, alongside rivers and streams in the New Forest.

leasehold About 30% of Forestry Commission land in England is leasehold and, as well as being time constrained, leases often carry other constraints: often, retention of shooting rights and restrictions on public access. Whilst all FC freehold land (*see also* freehold) has open public access, many leaseholds do not and they have made up a significant proportion of FC land sold since 1979.

MAFF (Ministry of Agriculture, Fisheries and Food) The agriculture ministry which now forms the larger part of Defra.

natural regeneration The regeneration of new trees, often after felling for timber, from seed on the site. Less intrusive than planting, natural regeneration can be patchy and unreliable.

Glossary

NCC (Nature Conservancy Council) The government's first nature conservation body, broken up into countries in 1988 as a result of the 'Flow Country' dispute.
NDR (Net Discounted Revenue) A modelling tool for predicting economic performance over time.
NE (Natural England) Formed from English Nature, the Countryside Agency and the Rural Development Agency in 2006 as the government's conservation and rural agency.
NFU (National Farmer's Union) Principle representative body for farming in England: in contrast to other Unions, it represents often wealthy land owning farmers, rather than employees
NGO (Non-Governmental Organisation) Organisations outside of government delivering public benefits, as providers or influencers of policy. Many are charities, including for the purpose of this book bodies such as the Woodland Trust, RSPB and National Trust
normal forest A forest where the ages of the stands of trees are spread across time to produce a constant supply of timber.
NWRDA (North West Regional Development Agency) One of the national network of nine regional agencies charged primarily with stimulating economic regeneration; established in 1998 and abolished in 2010.

ODPM (Office of the Deputy Prime Minister) Local Government Ministry under DPM John Prescott from 2001 to 2006; replaced by DCLG.

pasture woodland A historic woodland-management system where animals were allowed to graze under trees which were cut only above grazing reach. Cut limbs would be used for firewood and timber and the animals would feed on the foliage.
PAWS (Plantation on Ancient Woodland Sites) Ancient woodlands which have been planted with a tree species not native to the site, such as non-native conifers.
PEFC (Pan European Forest Certification) An alternative timber-certification organisation to FSC, arguably less guaranteed than FSC because rules are set by producers. In the UK both FSC and PEFC abide by the same standard, UKWAS.
PFE (Public Forest Estate) Term currently used by government to describe Forestry Commission land.
pinetum An arboretum devoted principally to coniferous trees.
planting Generally used in the sense of planting young trees reared in a forest nursery (as opposed to natural regeneration).
pollard Cutting a tree above the reach of grazing animals in a pasture woodland.
provenance Where a tree comes from in a geographical sense. Even within species this may mean significant differences in aspects like growth form (how straight the trunk, how branchy, for example), response to weather including frost hardiness etc.

raised bogs Deep peat bogs where the crown of the bog is raised above the base. There may be pool systems on the crown, as in the 'Flow Country'.
Ramsar International wetlands treaty signed in Ramsar, Iran, in 1962 which provides for legal designation of internationally important wetlands.
restocking Regeneration of a forest site after felling, generally by planting young trees raised in a forest nursery.
RHI (Renewable Heat Incentive) Government green energy scheme which pays a subsidy for heat production from a range of sources including wood. In line with the Woodfuel Strategy, it is aimed at small to medium, local-use heat.
RSPB (Royal Society for the Protection of Birds) The leading bird-conservation charity in the UK, with over a million members.
runoff Water running off the land when it rains, as opposed to soaking into the soil or evaporating.

SAC (Special Area of Conservation) Designation for sites selected under the EU Habitats Directive.
scarifier A machine, usually with rolling discs, sometimes with tines, which makes bare patches for restocking on bare forest after felling.
shelterwood A silvicultural system that is widely used in France to grow Oak where, at felling, a number of selected seed trees are left to re-populate the site with young trees through natural regeneration, after which the seed trees are felled.
silviculture The way in which trees are managed, generally to produce timber but also for other objectives. Includes differing approaches to species selection, thinning, felling and regeneration.
skidding Dragging logs out behind a winch tractor.
SPA (Special Protection Area) Land designated under the EU Birds Directive.
SSSI (Site of Special Scientific Interest) Legal designation of land of conservation interest, including nature and geology.
standards Single-stemmed trees left in a coppice to grow on to timber size.
SUDS (Sustainable Urban Drainage Schemes) Methods for mitigating local flooding in towns and cities including making hard surfaces more porous to absorb heavy rain fall – green roofs, porous surfaces to roads and driveways.

terminal height The height at which trees are likely to blow over on sites vulnerable to endemic wind throw.
thinning Removing some trees so others can grow on; critical to allowing the 'final crop' trees to gain maximum size and therefore value. Other than species selection at planting, thinning is the most important tool the forester has to manipulate a stand of trees to achieve his objectives.
Tree Council A partnership organisation promoting trees in general and urban tree planting and management in particular.

Glossary

UKFPA (United Kingdom Forest Products Association) Representative body of the larger UK forestry-processing companies, including sawmills and board mills.

UKWAS (UK Woodland Assurance Scheme) The agreed standard for forest certification in the UK.

valley mires Peat bogs along the bottom of valleys, with most surviving examples occurring in the New Forest.

windthrow / wind-blow Trees blown over by gales. 'Catastrophic' windthrow, which can blow over almost any tree, is best known, with the famous 1987 storm in southeast England the most recent example. However, for foresters 'endemic windthrow' where trees in the uplands on wet soils are blown over by normal winter gales once they reach a certain height (depending on the individual site) is more serious, if less dramatic.

yield class Measure of timber growth. Trees have an s-shaped growth pattern – slow at first, then faster and faster, before tailing off as old age approaches. Yield class measures the cubic metres produced per hectare at the point where the trees are growing fastest; for native broadleaves, a range of 4–8, Scots Pine 8–12, spruces and firs 10–18.

Index

(*See also* People Index p214 *and* Place Index p217)

38 Degrees petition 5, 165

access history 49
acidification 31
activity centres 151
Agriculture Act 1947 189
Allerdale District Council 136
Ancient and Ornamental woodland (A&O) 107, 110, 114, 115, 120
Ancient Woodland Project 79-80
ancient woodland/woods 15, 69-70, 72, 73, 74, 75, 76, 77, 78, 79, 80, 83,
Apical track shoes 27
art projects in forests 22, 51-2, 65
Ash disease 80, 184
Atlantic Oakwoods EU Life project 40

B&Q 94, 96
Banks Mining 143
'Big society' 5, 116, 166
biodiversity 199
Biomass Energy Centre 160
bird boxes 38
bogs 14
boilers 161-2
British Trust for Ornithology (BTO)/national survey 39, 44
brunchorstia 15
Butterfly Conservation 81, 88

Capital Modernisation Fund (CMF) 55, 144, 146
car parking/parks 22, 49, 50, 52, 56, 58, 66, 113
carbon/carbon issues 157, 158, 196-7

Civil service/servants 7, 122, 123, 130, 131, 134, 169, 177, 180, 186
climate change 63, 163, 196
Climate Change Adaptation Panel 135
coalfield restoration 140, 141, 144, 145
coastal sand dune systems 36
commercial woods (red) 105-6
Common Ground 47
common rights 108, 112
commoners 113
Commoners Defence Association 112
commoning 107-8
community representation 186, 187
community forests/woods 112, 193
concerts 138
Confor 158, 163, 175
conservancies 123, 124
conservation 72, 73, 190
conservation committees 40
conservation problems 81-2
conservation projects 69
conservationists 100
continuous cover 97
coppices/coppicing 70-1, 72, 76, 81, 82
Country Land and Business Association (CLA) 160
Country Landowners' Association 171
country parks 54-5, 57, 67
Countryside Agency 183
Countryside and Rights of Way Act 2000 (CRoW) 6, 112, 166

210

Index

Countryside Commission 133, 140
Countryside Council for Wales 36
cycling/cycle trails 58, 59, 60, 152

Dean sculpture trail 65
deer 11, 20, 37-8, 81, 82, 90, 108, 109
deer lawns 23
Deer Removal Act 1851 112
Department for Environment, Food & Rural Affairs (Defra) 7, 89, 131, 132, 133, 142, 159, 160, 165, 169-70, 171, 177, 178, 179, 181, 182, 183, 184, 185, 186, 188, 199
Department for Energy & Climate Change (DECC) 160
Department for the Communities & Local Government (DCLG) 142
Department of Agriculture for Scotland (Dafs) 26
Department for the Environment, Transport & the Regions (DETR) 142
devolution 124
Diver islands 39
dog swimming pond 145
Doncaster Earth Centre Millennium Lottery project 51
draining 31
dung counts 38

East Dorset District Council 57
Economic Forestry Group 23
Economics for the Environment Consultancy (Eftec) 105, 175, 191, 192, 196
Edgelands 141, 142, 146
encapsulated signs 43
England Forestry Strategy 140
English community forests 140
English National Forestry Forum 179
English Nature 78, 79, 88, 89, 118, 133 (*see also* Natural England)

Environment Agency 120, 153, 183
Environmental site planning 42
Esso/Esso Trees of Time and Place project 115, 119
EU LIFE projects 40, 87, 89, 119, 120

Farming & Wildlife Advisory Group (FWAG) 33
felling 17, 19, 21, 43, 48, 68, 81, 83, 99-100
fires 12
flooding 192
flooding crisis (2014) 189, 191
floods (2007) 192
'Flow Country' 9-29, 49, 87, 92, 94, 124, 169, 199
Food and Environment Research Agency (FERA) 185
food security campaign 189
Foot and Mouth disease 134-7, 139
Ford Country Tractors 17
Foresight Review of Flooding 192
forest certification 94, 95, 96
Forest Distinctiveness 47
forest districts 123
forest drives 21-2
forest hazards 12
Forest Holidays 178
forest ownership 5-6
Forest Research 143, 160
forest restrictions 5
forest rights 5
Forest Services 183, 184
forest walks 50
foresters 8, 23
forestry equipment 42
Forestry Stewardship Council (FSC) 6, 79, 94, 95
Fountain Forestry 20, 26
fracking 187
freehold estates 5-6
furniture 53, 54

211

Index

'garden cities' 193
German U-boat campaign (1917) 9
GM crops 187
Go Ape 138, 139, 151, 152
government agency reviews 182-3
grant rules 33
Green Arc 154
Green Belt 142, 163, 193
Guardians 176, 177-8

habitat restoration 157, 158
Halliburton 189
Hampshire Wildlife Trust 112
Health and Safety Executive (HSE) 58
heathland 76, 77, 84-5, 86-7, 107
herbicides 14
heritage forests 166
Heritage Lottery Fund (HLF) 65, 67, 155, 156
Herpetological Conservation Trust (HCT) 85, 86
Higher Level Stewardship 90, 132
House of Commons 6
HS2 (High Speed 2 railway line) 187

Impact Assessment 167
Independent Forestry Panel (IFP) 173, 175, 176, 177, 179, 186, 191, 194, 201
information leaflets 50
Institute of Terrestrial Ecology (ITE) 36
International Year of the Environment (IYE) 34, 39

land sales programme 106
landscape plans 43
landscapes 24
landscaping 46, 49
landuse 48, 174, 189, 190, 192, 193, 199, 200, 201
leasehold estates 5
limestone pavement 88

logging (USA) 41
low carbon economy 163
lowland heath 5

Ministry of Agriculture, Fisheries & Food (MAFF) 92, 130, 140, 142, 183
Major Landowners Group 89
management of FC 125-33
management tables 19
media communication 67-8
Mersey Forest 147
mining timber 18-19
Ministry of Defence (MoD) 87, 89, 90
mountain bikes/biking 58-9, 60, 61

National Farmers Union (NFU) 189
national forests 140
National Household Survey 50-1, 56
national nature reserves 133
National Pinetum 64-5
National Trust (NT) 6, 54, 84, 100, 156, 166, 167, 168
Natural England 90, 132, 156, 183
Nature Conservancy Council (NCC) 17, 24, 27, 28, 29, 39, 113
Nature Conservation 17
Nature Conservation Guidelines 43
Nature Conservation Review 26
nature trail leaflets 65
nature trails 50
nesting projects 38, 39
net discounted revenue 15, 21
New Forest Acts 114, 115
New Forest Dog 112
New Forest New Future Project 116, 118, 119
Newlands 127, 147
North East Conservancy 20
North West Regional Development Agency (NWRDA) 146, 147, 150
nurseries 13

Index

Open Forest 107
Operations Instruction 1 42
organisation of FC 122-5
Our Forests (ginger group) 173, 176

pannage 109
'parklands' concept 153
pasture woodland 71-2, 107
paths 55
peri-urban programme 189
peri-urban woods 148, 149
pests 20
phosphate fertiliser 16
picnic tables 22
plantable reserve 12
Plantations on Ancient Woodland Sites (PAWS) 73, 75, 166
planting 12, 13, 14, 15, 16, 17, 33, 140
planting, upland 9-10, 29
play trails 57, 58, 59, 61
ploughing 13, 20, 21, 31
policy, broadleaves 32, 34
pollarding 71-2, 110
Private Finance Initiative (PFI) 152
privatisation
   (1993-4) 92-3, 103-4
   (2010-11) 5-7, 80, 93, 165-72
Public Forest Estate (PFE) 177, 178, 179, 188
public relations 67

Ramblers 92, 158
recreation 49-68
refreshments 51
regeneration 97
renewable energy 158-9, 160
Renewable Heat Incentive (RHI) 161, 162, 197
restocking 20
restoration 75, 76, 80, 85, 86, 91, 117, 119, 143, 166, 211
restoration sites 147, 157

restructuring 43-4, 45, 47, 48
rotations 44
Royal Society for the Protection of Birds (RSPB) 24, 27, 32, 33-4, 35, 38, 40, 54, 80, 87, 90, 106, 118, 149, 153, 154, 157, 166, 183

Save our Woods website 186
Scottish Office 17, 29,
sculpture (outdoors) 51, 52-3, 66
sheep farming 26
silviculture 18, 48, 97
site-planning systems 42, 95
Sites of Special Scientific Interest (SSSIs) 17, 25, 26, 30
Small Woods Association 195
social media campaigns 186
Soil Association 94
spades, semi-circular 13
Sports Council England 151
SSSIs 88, 89, 90
Survival Anglia 28
Sutton Wildlife Trust 15
Swedish scarifiers 21

tax reliefs/concessions 26, 29
temporary operations signs 43
terminal height (trees) 19
thinning 17-18, 19, 47, 81, 82, 97, 98
threshold signs 50
timber enclosures 110
timber forests 36
timber value 16, 99, 101
Times, The 5
toilets 50, 51, 52
Tree Council/tree wardens 194
tree diseases 63, 101-2, 184, 195-6
tree growth 62
tree shelters 33

UK Forest Products Association (UKFPA) 101, 163, 167, 175

Index

UK Woodland Assurance Scheme (UKWAS) 6, 167, 170
United Utilities 156
upland grass 12
USA experience/Forest Service 24, 41, 42, 67, 94

Verderers of the New Forest/Verderers enclosures 111, 112, 115, 116, 180
visitor attractions/centres/events/facilities 50, 51, 53, 138, 139, 151, 152

Wasteland to Woodlands programme 144
water issues 30-1
water management 154
waymarking 56
West Highland Survey 16

Westonbirt, Friends of 63, 64
wind farms 187
wind issues 19
windthrow 43, 45, 47, 48
wood boilers 161-2, 164
Wood Production Outlook 24
woodfuel strategy 159, 161, 164
woodland culture 194, 201
Woodland Trust 6, 74, 80, 81, 83, 84, 149, 153, 158, 166, 167, 168, 183, 184, 194
woods, sales of 103, 104
 see also privatisation
Worcestershire County Council 159
Work Study (operational research branch) 21
World Wildlife Fund (WWF) 95

Yield class 10

People Index

Abbot, Mike 194
Anderson, Hen 186
Anderson, John 53
Angus, Hugh 62
Ashmole, Mike 20
Avery, Mark 29

Barber, Derek 140
Barlow, Arthur 114, 115, 116, 119
Bell, Simon 41
Bellamy, David 28
Berzins, Andy 53
Bibby, Colin 34
Bills, David 95

Boyd, Ian 184
Boyd, Morton 40
Brown, Nick 120
Burlton, Bill 87
Busby, Roger 85, 94, 95, 97, 124

Caborn, Richard 151
Calder, Sandy 14, 21, 27
Cameron, David 5, 6, 147, 173
Campbell, Duncan 24, 41
Canterbury, Archbishop of 5
Carter, Susan 134, 135
Chard, Jack 22
Clare, John 112

People Index

Clark, David (Lord Clark of Windermere) 30, 131-2, 151
Clarke, Peter 32
Corbett, Keith 85
Corrigan, Chris 118
Crowburn, Rebecca 159, 160
Crowe, Dame Sylvia 24, 117
Currie, Fred 37, 75

Daniels, Rich 186, 187
Davies, Ron 32
Dench, Dame Judi 5
Dennis, Roy 38, 39
Dhanak, Mittesh 148
Dickie, Ian 175
Duignan, Angela 161

Evans, Julian 103
Everard, John 97
Eves, Alan 139

Farley, Paul 60
Farrell, Terry Sir 153
Ferguson, Tom 143
Field, Alison 119
Francis, Gwynn 28
Fraser-Darling, Frank 16
Frost, Andy 57, 58
Fryer-Spedding family 136

Gill, Graham 61, 87
Gill, Sir Ben 158, 159, 160
Gissop, Gerry 59
Goldsworthy, Andy 51
Grant, Bill 22, 53
Green, Ted 78
Greig, Sandy 143

Hall, Andy 159
Hamilton, Frank 26
Harding, Brian 89
Harding, Emma 160

Harwood, Oliver 160
Haskins, Lord 132, 133, 134
Hatfield, Geoff 126, 138, 141
Haw, Geoff 45
Hayden, Paul 194
Heath, David 173
Henderson, Mike 98
Hoblyn, Ron 52
Hodges, Tim 80
Holden, Sue 80
Holme, George 30
Hough, Mike 145

Jackson, Dorothy 94
Jeffries, Katrina 128
Jones, James (Bishop of Liverpool) 173, 176

Keen, Paula 75
Kennedy, John 34
Kirby, Keith 79, 115
Knight, Alan 94, 96

Leatherdale, Simon 75
Leitz, Gudrun 194
Lucas, Oliver 24, 46, 57, 94
Lyon, Jim 138

Mahony, Brian 98
Mason, Anne 186
Mattingley, Alan 92
Mayhew, Crispin 138
McCreagh, Mary 168
McIntosh, Bob 43, 75, 98, 144
Meehan, John 143
Meeks, Steve 128
Moffat, Andy 143
Morley, Elliot 120, 136
Morrison, Sandy 32

Nash, David 66
Nolan, Paul 147

People Index

Orram, Martin 51

Paice, Jim 96, 165, 166, 167, 168, 170, 171, 173
Passmore, Anthony 112
Paterson, Owen 173, 182, 184, 189
Pennistan, Morley 22
Perry, David 114
Peterken, George 32, 70, 78, 83, 84, 115
Petty, Steve 36-7
Phillips, Adrian 140
Porritt, Jonathon 6, 168, 173
Prescott, John 142, 149
Prest, Graeme 136
Prince of Wales 9-10
Pryor, Simon 79

Quelch, Peter 39

Rabagliati, Jane 90
Rackham, Oliver 32, 70, 72, 74, 75, 78, 195
Rantzen, Esther
Ratcliffe, Derek 24
Ratcliffe, Phil 37, 38
Rees, Jeremy 51
Reynolds, Fiona 168
Reynolds, Martin 146, 150
Robinson, Chris 144, 145
Rogerson, Dan 173, 179, 182
Rollinson, Tim 140
Rose, Ronnie 23
Rothnie, Bruce 116
Rowan, Alastair 27
Russell, Henry 194-5
Russell, Tony 63

Sawyer, Tim 97
Scott, Alastair 34

Seddon, Mike 116
Sharland, Richard 143-4
Shepherd, Gillian 92
Small, Don 113
Spain, Marion 153-4
Spelman, Caroline 166, 167, 168, 170, 173
Spencer, Jonathan 75, 76, 78, 90, 115
Spencer, Tony 43
Stern, Rod 85
Stevenson, Alan 39, 144
Stockdale, Brian 45
Swabey, James 49, 52, 53, 58, 59, 65, 116, 145
Swayne, Desmond 121
Symmons Roberts, Michael 60

Tabbush, Paul 20
Taylor, Mike 138
Tewson, John 141
Thompson, Donald 116, 120, 134, 135-6
Thornycroft, Mark 106
Thorpe, David 145
Titchmarsh, Alan 65
Tubbs, Colin 113
Tubby Ian, 160

Warren, Martin 88
Watson, Peter 90
Watts, Joe 143
White, John 62
Widget, Nigel 59
Williamson, David 54, 81, 98
Wilson, Andy 139
Wogan, Sir Terry 26
Wormell, Peter 39
Worthington, Roger 117, 118
Wright, Russell 118

Place Index

Abernethy 32
Arnolfini Centre for Contemporary
  Arts, Bristol 51
Avalon Marshes, Somerset 156

Bassenthwaite Water 136, 137
Bedgebury, Kent 60, 62, 64-5
Beechenhurst 52, 53
Bernewood, Oxon 46, 82
Berwyns, Wales 24
Blean Forest, North East Kent 81
Bradfield Woods 15
Brecks, Thetford Forest 9
British Columbia, Canada 41

Cairngorms 32
Cannock 59
Cardinham, Cornwall 106
Chopwell, Co Durham 61
Clipstone Forest 199-200
Cornwall, Duchy of 10
Creag Meagaidh 25, 26
Crooksbury Common, Surrey 85
Cumbria 137

Dalavich Oakwood, Argyll 39, 75
Dalby (Forest/Valley) 17, 21-2, 45, 50,
  59, 105, 106, 139, 153
Dartmoor forests 10
Dean Forest Park 52
Dean Sculpture Trail 51
Delamere, Cheshire 178
Dodd Wood 136, 137
Dorset Heaths 16, 85
Dumfries and Galloway 16

Dunwich, Suffolk 106

East Anglia 15
Ennerdale Project 156
Epping Forest 154
Eskdalemuir Forest 23

Falling Fosse 14
Fineshade, Northhants 80, 178
'Flow Country' 7, 12, 25, 26, 27, 28,
  34, 49, 94
Forest of Dean 49, 52, 59, 92, 97, 134,
  166, 178, 186

Grizedale/Grizedale Forest 22, 47, 51,
  57

Haldon Play trail, Exeter 61
Hampton Development,
  Peterborough 194
Harwood Forest 19
Haugh Wood 46
High Lodge Visitor Centre, East
  Anglia 138

Ingrebourne Hill 145-6

Jeskyns Wood 145, 148, 149, 154

Kielder/Kielder Forest 19, 20, 36, 37,
  43, 44, 45, 47, 48, 87, 88, 105

Lake District/Lake District National
  Park 17, 47, 57, 88, 136
Langdale 22, 106

217

Place Index

Lavenham 74-5

Marches, The 104
May Moss 14
Moors Valley, Bournemouth 57, 58, 138, 139
Mostyn Vale 147

Neroche Forest, Blackdowns 155, 156
Neroche Forest, Somerset Blackdown Hills 105
New Forest, The 5, 86, 89, 92, 107-21, 134, 135, 155, 157, 166
Newborough Forest, Anglesey 36
Newtondale 45
Nightingale Wood, Swindon 140
Northhants 78-9
North West England 22
North Yorks Moors 14, 15, 18
North Yorkshire 15, 17
 (*see also* Yorkshire)
Northumberland 13, 19, 44
Nottinghamshire 141

Oregon, Washington, USA 41
Orlestone Forest, Kent 75, 82
Overscourt, Forest of Avon 140

Rendlesham 106
Rewell Wood, Sussex 81
Rigg Wood, Lake District 105

Rosliston 140
Salisbury Plain 89
Savernake Forest, Wiltshire 78
Somerset Levels 189
South and West England Region 42
Staindale Lake 22
Sutton Manor 150

Thames Chase 145, 146
Thames Gateway 143, 148, 153
Thetford 105
Thetford Bird Trail 52
Thetford Forest Special Protection Area 48
Thetford Forest/Project 9, 15, 34, 36, 48, 186

Uswayford 9, 13

Viridor Wood 145

Wareham Forest, Dorset 85
Westonbirt Arboretum 53, 62, 63, 64, 153
Whinlatter Visitor Centre 136, 137, 139
Wykeham 21
Wyre Visitor Centre/Forest 51, 55, 77

Yorkshire 14, 19, 20, 21, 45
 (*see also* North Yorkshire)